We Will Pray *for* Election Day

Thomas Freiling &
Michael Klassen

Allegiance Press
The Right Answers for America

We Will Pray for Election Day
by Thomas Freiling and Michael Klassen

Printed in the United States of America

ISBN 1-594671-79-6

Allegiance Press
10640 Main Street
Suite 204
Fairfax, VA 22030
www.allegiancepress.com

(703) 934-4411

"The time has come that Christians must vote for honest men, and take a consistent ground in politics. God cannot sustain this free and blessed country, which we love and pray for, unless the Church will take right ground. Politics are a part of a religion in such a country as this, and Christians must do their duty to the country as a part of their duty to God. It seems sometimes as if the foundations of the nation are becoming rotten, and Christians seem to act as if they think God does not see what they do in politics. But I tell you He does see it, and He will bless or curse this nation, according to the course they take."

—Charles Finney (1792-1875)

Table of Contents

Introduction

Why We Must Pray

Only four years have passed since the *surreal* general election of 2000 when millions of Americans were given a crash course in civic law. For the first time in our generation we went to bed on election night perplexed about who would be the next president of the United States. This was one of the closest general elections in U.S. history.

People knew that the race would be close – but not this close! Tight races in Iowa, New Hampshire, New Mexico, Oregon, and Wisconsin cast doubt on whether a decisive victor would be determined. Television networks eager to declare a winner initially projected Vice President Al Gore as the next president, then retracted their declarations when the count became indiscernibly close. Late into the night (or make that early into the morning) one fact became clear: the battlefield for the 43rd president of the United States would be fought in the state of Florida.

Hanging chads, miscounted votes, and alleged racial and age discrimination at the polls heightened the tensions not only in Florida, but across the United States. Ironically, the governor of the state of Florida also happened to be the brother of the Republican candidate — Texas Governor George Bush.

So the people of the United States waited for six weeks

while the election chaos was sorted out. Some pundits wondered whether America was experiencing a constitutional crisis.

After vote recounts and court decisions that extended all the way to the Supreme Court, the picture hardly seemed clear: Al Gore won the popular vote by only 543,614 votes, a difference of half a percent, over his opponent George Bush. George Bush, on the other hand, won the electoral vote 271 to 266. According to the Constitution of the United States, the candidate with the most electoral votes wins.

George W. Bush became only the second president in U.S. history to lose the popular vote and still take office because he had garnered the electoral vote.

But consider this:

- A change in only 269 votes in the state of Florida would have given the election to Vice President Al Gore.
- A change of only 5,381 votes in four states would have resulted in *neither* candidate gaining the majority. At that point, the House of Representatives would have elected our next president!

During those uneasy days, democracy seemed to hang like a chad on an election ballot. Would our Constitution hold our country together? Would the American people follow a president who failed to win the popular vote?

Every Vote Counts

One lesson we learned as a result of the 2000 elections is that every vote counts — whether on the national level or on the local level. Only 269 votes in the state of Florida made the difference in our next president!

Seemingly innocuous elections can determine the course our nation takes for the next two to four years.

Perhaps even beyond that. Consider the kinds of decisions our elected officials make:

- Nomination and ratification of the Supreme Court and State Supreme Court justices
- Legislation that defines what constitutes a family and what constitutes a viable human life (at birth or at the end of life)
- Tax and economic determinations that dramatically affect the rich and poor
- Decrees that ensure our freedom to worship God and to share our faith in Jesus Christ with those around us

From a Christian worldview, the role of government is to restrain sin. In a secular society we don't expect government to legislate our faith, but at the same time, we don't expect it to restrain it as it should restrain sin.

In his travels we know that the Apostle Paul encouraged believers to pray for those in authority over them:

> *I urge, then, first of all, that requests, prayers, intercession and thanksgiving be made for everyone—for kings and all those in authority, that we may live peaceful and quiet lives in all godliness and holiness. This is good, and pleases God our Savior, who wants all men to be saved and to come to a knowledge of the truth.*
>
> *1 Timothy 2:1-4*

Dictates, proclamations, and decisions by kings and all those in authority (many of whom were elected by the people) created an environment in which peace, godliness, and holiness could flourish. This was also fertile soil in which the gospel could thrive.

Our Voting Record Reveals a Great Deal About Us

By virtue of being elected by the people, our governmental authorities represent us – our beliefs, our likes and dislikes, our definition of sin and righteousness.

Not only should we pray then for our elected officials, it goes without saying that we should pray for discernment among the voting public. How can we know which candidate will represent us best? Proverbs 14:34 tells us that "Righteousness exalts a nation." Which candidate will govern us in righteousness?

This begs the question: what should you – and the rest of the American voting public – do with your vote on November 2, 2004?

Why We Must Pray

The purpose of *We Will Pray for Election Day* is to mobilize the body of Christ to pray for the November 2, 2004, general election. Our desire is that this book will help activate 1 million prayer activists to pray as one for God's kingdom to come and His will to be done in the upcoming election.

In order for this to happen, it's going to take more than a book. While this book will serve as a helpful tool, what's more important is that we find a way to bring the body of Christ together – regardless of party affiliation – to pray.

Prayer isn't a formula we use to strong-arm God into following our wishes. But something happens when we gather to pray. Something powerful, something supernatural. And sometimes when we pray we discover that we are joining God in His work. Here's what Jesus said about prayer:

> *Again, I tell you that if two of you on earth agree about anything you ask for, it will be done for you by my Father in heaven. For where two or three come together in my*

> *name, there am I with them.*
>
> *Matthew 18:19-20*

When as few as two or three of Jesus' followers gather together in His name, Jesus becomes mysteriously present. Granted, Jesus is present when we pray by ourselves and for ourselves, but something special happens when the body of Christ joins together in prayer.

Corporate prayer adds something that individual prayer cannot. And when corporate prayer intersects with God's will, amazing things take place. But just because we gather together in prayer doesn't mean we'll get what we ask for. Jesus explained,

> *If you remain in me and my words remain in you, ask whatever you wish, and it will be given you.*
>
> *John 15:7*

To remain in Christ implies intimacy. As we deepen our walk with Jesus, He changes our desires. He conforms our prayers to His will. We join God in His work.

Isn't that your desire for the upcoming election?

How to Use This Book

The prayers in *We Will Pray for Election Day* are divided into four areas.

Prayers of Adoration and Thanksgiving are intended to bring perspective. Before presenting our requests to God, why not spend a moment enjoying Him and acknowledging His power and love? After all, prayer isn't just about asking, it's also about worship, intimacy, knowing God.

Prayers for the Election Process deal with candidates, campaigning, and the election itself. Let's be honest: all too often a campaign message is lost in a chaotic mess of scandals, accusations, or hype. We need eyes to see the true candidate and ears to hear the true message of a campaign. We also need fair elections and candidates who are kept safe throughout the process.

Prayers for Issues address important issues that stand behind many of the candidates and referendums on the November ballot. But praying for issues falls short without the next area.

Prayers for the Hearts of the American People are prayers for the voters. The hearts of the American people are at the core of what we are praying for. America is changed not through legislation but through transformation.

These prayers aren't magical incantations. They're simply a guide to help you pray and to provide a framework for you to join your prayers with thousands, perhaps millions, of others.

Taking Action

Chuck Colson once said, "We should always pray with as much earnestness as those who expect everything from God; we should always act with as much energy as those who expect everything from themselves." Indeed, faith without works is dead!

So in addition to praying for our country and the upcoming election, we are equipping you to take action and make a difference in 2004. After each prayer we give you ideas on how to get involved — from helping register people to vote to working on behalf of a candidate running for office. You are also given an election timeline, a voter registration guide, a summary of key political races in 2004, and additional voter resources.

Just because you are a Christian does not mean you shouldn't get involved in politics. On the contrary, it's because you believe in God and His authority *over* government that you *should* get involved. When the Apostle Paul was restricted from preaching the gospel, he appealed to the highest court in the Roman Empire — the infamous Emperor Nero (Acts 25)! In the same way, we shouldn't be afraid to enter the political arena for the sake of the gospel.

Our political leaders set the standard of morality by the laws they create and enforce. For example, they are the ones who will decide if unborn babies will live or die, if the institution of marriage will be upheld, and how the poor and defenseless are cared for.

Proverbs says, "When rulers are wicked, their people are too; but good men will live to see the tyrant's downfall" (Proverbs 29:16 TLB). When the moral, God-fearing people of our country do not take responsibility for our government, we leave the doors open for our nation to be governed by the immoral and amoral.

So don't sit on the sidelines! It's important that we pray — but also important that we vote and involve ourselves in the voting process.

God Is on God's Side

Joshua had just led the Israelites across the Jordan River on dry land. The adult males had been circumcised again, and they were about to overtake the walled city of Jericho as the first step in taking possession of the Promised Land. But before mobilizing the Israelite army, the commander of the Lord's army appeared before Joshua.

"Are you for us or for our enemies?" Joshua asked the man whom many scholars believe was the preincarnate Christ.

Many of us would expect the commander of the Lord's army to reply, "I am sent to go before God's chosen people to lead them into the Promised Land." But that wasn't His answer.

"Are you for us or for our enemies?"

The next best guess would be for the commander to

answer, "I am for both you and your enemies." But that's not what he said.

"Are you for us or for our enemies?"

Obviously, the commander didn't answer, "I am for your enemies." God didn't lead the Israelites into the Promised Land only to oppose them.

"Are you for us or for our enemies?"

> *"Neither," he replied, "but as commander of the army of the Lord I have now come." Then Joshua fell facedown to the ground in reverence, and asked him, "What message does my Lord have for his servant?" The commander of the Lord's army replied, "Take off your sandals, for the place where you are standing is holy." And Joshua did so.*
>
> *Joshua 5:14-15*

Did you catch that? At the moment in Israel's history when you would most expect God to take sides, He doesn't.

So whose side is God on? Neither. God is on God's side. When Israel chose to join God, they enjoyed the fruit of God's blessing. When they strayed from God, they tasted the bitter fruit of their own sin.

In this upcoming election, let's not pray for God to join our side or assume that He's already on our side. Rather, let's pray, "God, give us Your heart. Show us Your way. Help us to know where You are so we can join You in Your work and taste the fruit of Your blessing."

This is a good time to follow Joshua's lead. Let's fall facedown to the ground in reverence and ask God, "What message do You have for Your servant?"

Now let's pray!

Prayers of Adoration and Thanksgiving

Prayer 1

Declaring God's Dominion Over the Election

Oh, the depth of the riches and wisdom and knowledge of God! How unsearchable are his judgments and how inscrutable his ways! "For who has known the mind of the Lord, or who has been his counselor?" "Or who has given a gift to him that he might be repaid?" For from him and through him and to him are all things. To him be glory forever. Amen.

Romans 11:33-36 ESV

Almighty God,

With confidence I proclaim Your unparalleled dominion over all the nations of the earth including the United States of America. From Your holy throne You rule over our nation, and by Your hand You raise up our leaders and take them down. "The king's heart is like a stream of water directed by the Lord; he turns it wherever he pleases."

Your power extends over the legislatures, judicial courts, national affairs, daily events, and even the trivial nuances of my life. You were there before the foundations of our country were laid, and Your power continues throughout eternity. You are stronger than any president, wiser than any judge, and greater than my heart.

Not even the powers of darkness can overcome the light of Your glory. And at the end of the age "every knee will bow in heaven and on earth and under the earth, and every tongue confess that Jesus is Lord to the glory of God the Father."

I praise You because Your wisdom is beyond comprehension and Your understanding has no limit. As the heavens are higher than the earth, so are Your ways higher than our ways and Your thoughts higher than our thoughts. All human wisdom belongs to You and derives from You.

In a world that indiscriminately redefines truth, You are the plumb line that never changes. You are the author of truth, and Your Son Jesus embodies Your truth.

Not only are You all-powerful and all-wise and the definition of truth, but You are trustworthy. You are faithful in all You do. Everything You do is right, and all Your ways are just.

Because You are in complete control, I don't need to fear the outcome of the upcoming elections. Because You are greater than our hearts, You know everything. Despite our misguided zeal, our ill-informed decisions, and our personal agendas, we know that You work out everything in conformity with the purpose of Your will. Thank You that our fate doesn't lie solely in the ballot box. Through my prayers I choose to join You in Your work.

This I know and in this I can take comfort: Your kingdom will come and Your will *will* be done on earth as it is in heaven.

Scripture references: Job 38:4; Psalm 33:4, 47:8, 139:6, 147:5; Proverbs 21:1 (NLT); Isaiah 55:9; Daniel 4:37; Matthew 6:10; Ephesians 1:11; Philippians 2:9-11 (NIV); 1 John 3:20

Join 1 million prayer activists

We are asking 1 million patriotic Americans to pray for the upcoming election. If you agree to join with us in prayer, please visit our website, www.TheChristianVote.org, and sign up to be a prayer activist. We'll send you free weekly prayer campaign alerts and show you how to get a copy of this important book to your friends and family.

> *I know not how long a republican government can flourish among a great people who have not the Bible; the experiment has never been tried; but this I do know: that the existing government of this country never could have had existence but for the Bible.*
>
> *—William Henry Seward, 1836*

Prayer 2

Acknowledging God's Holiness and Love

The Word became flesh and made his dwelling among us. We have seen his glory, the glory of the One and Only, who came from the Father, full of grace and truth.

John 1:14 NIV

Almighty God,

You are holy. Your perfection sets You apart from me, and Your inherent justice demands that all sin be punished — including mine. No one is like You, and there is no one besides You. Everything You do reflects who You are — Your works are perfect and all Your ways are just. Righteousness, justice, and truth find their definitions in You. You are light, and in You is no darkness at all.

When I see myself in the light of Your holiness I can't help but respond like Simon Peter: "Go away from me, Lord; I am a sinful man!"

If You were only holy, where would I go to rid myself of this sin-sickness that plagues everything I do? How could I know this holy God when I am so beset by sin?

Although You are completely holy, You are also love. "Your love, O Lord, reaches to the heavens, your faithfulness to the skies." Your love is inescapable. Even if I stray to the ends of the earth, I cannot outrun Your great love. You are gracious and merciful, slow to anger and abounding in steadfast love.

Your set-apartness shows me Your greatness, but Your love draws me closer to Your heart.

Your Son Jesus is the incarnation of Your love and holiness, Your grace and truth, Your mercy and justice. He who had no sin became sin for me so that in Him I might become the righteousness of God. And when He was nailed to the cross,

Jesus bore my sin so that I could know this holy God. Thank You for sending Your son to be the remedy for my sin-sickness.

My desire is to reveal the light of the One who lives in me — Jesus Christ. May the choices I make reflect the holiness and love of Your Son Jesus. And may I become a person who yearns for Your character. In the upcoming elections, please help me avoid decisions based on holiness devoid of love, or grace without truth.

Lord God, Your paradoxical ways prove that You are a mystery. Help me to live in this tension as I seek to know You and become more like You.

And may You move the American people to vote in a way that reflects both Your love and Your holiness.

Scripture references: Deuteronomy 32:41; 1 Samuel 2:2, 6:20; Psalm 36:5, 145:8 (ESV); Luke 5:8; John 1:5; 2 Corinthians 5:21

Register to vote, now

Many of us — more than 50 million citizens in this country — are eligible to vote but don't bother to register. If you are at least 18 years old, you may register to vote. In all but four states you must register before Election Day, and in many states you must register 30 days before an election. Don't wait! See the Voter Registration Guide on page 203 of this book and then contact your county or city government to find out where to register.

Let us look forward to the time when we can take the flag of our country and nail it below the Cross, and there let it wave as it waved in the olden times, and let us gather around it and inscribe for our motto: "Liberty and Union, one and inseparable, now and forever," and exclaim, Christ first, our country next!

—Andrew Johnson, 1875

Prayer 3

Thanking God for Giving Us the Mind of Christ

"For who has known the mind of the Lord that he may instruct him?" But we have the mind of Christ.

1 Corinthians 2:16

Almighty God,

As I reflect on the upcoming election, I feel bombarded by a myriad of choices: Which candidates do I vote for? What issues are *Your* issues? What seemingly trivial referendums may later come back to haunt us?

Despite my desire to vote in accordance with Your desires, I admit that on my own I am unable to do so. My flesh yearns for satisfaction. I'm so easily distracted by self-serving issues. And I have a fallen nature that is simply unable to clearly hear Your voice.

Thank You for giving me the mind of Christ. Your Spirit-led, peace-producing, God-loving, life-giving, truth-seeking wisdom resides in the deepest part of me. I don't even have to ask for the mind of Christ because You tell me in Your Word that I already have it! Because I am a new creation and my mind is already set on the things of the Spirit, I rejoice that life and peace reside in the core of who I am.

Jesus, You promised that when the Spirit comes, He will guide us into all truth. Thank You that Your Spirit *has* come and now resides in me! Your higher ways are part and parcel of my regenerated soul.

Because of this I don't need to fear the future. I don't need to get bogged down by anxieties about what might happen if my desires aren't reflected on Election Day. Your divine power has given me everything — everything! — I need for life and godliness through my knowledge of and relationship with You.

I acknowledge that I'm not God — but thank You for living in me! Thank You for giving me Your Spirit as a down payment on eternity.

I may see through a glass dimly, but I look forward to the day when I will see You face to face in all Your glory — on that day when I won't need to ask for wisdom because I will know fully what Your desires are. I will know You and I will be fully known.

But in the meantime I will walk in the knowledge that You reside in me and that You are already guiding me in Your eternal purposes. May I respond to the gentle promptings of Your Holy Spirit's call. And may the body of Christ in America vote in accordance with the wisdom You have already given them.

Scripture references: Jeremiah 31:34; John 16:13-15; Romans 8:5-9; 1 Corinthians 13:12; 2 Corinthians 5:17; 2 Peter 1:3

Register other people to vote

If we registered to vote just 1 percent of all the people who are still unregistered, 500,000 more votes would be cast on Election Day. Imagine the impact! Registering voters is easy. You could even set up a voter registration booth at your church or at a local Christian college. But remember: voter registration is a non-partisan activity, which means you must allow people to register for the political party of their choice. For further information, contact the Voter Registration and Education Project Information Center at Citizen Link, a part of Focus on the Family, at 800-232-6459.

There is a vital interrelationship between our prayers and American's future greatness. God wants to bless our land through the channels of our prayer. America's moral goodness and spiritual greatness and our success and prosperity are inseparable.

—Lloyd Ogilvie, 1992

Prayer 4

Thanking God for Freedom

After all, brothers, you were called to be free; do not use your freedom as an opening for self-indulgence, but be servants to one another in love.

Galatians 5:13 NJB

Almighty God,

For more than 200 hundred years, men and women of faith and courage have laid down their lives to secure freedom for this country. Blood was shed — and continues to be shed — so that Americans may enjoy liberty, democracy, and the freedom to worship without fear of reprisal.

Because I am free I can choose between candidates and issues in the upcoming election, I can vote according to my conscience, and I can voice my opinion. Because I am free I can choose my profession and I can worship according to my convictions. Because I am free I can share the good news of freedom in Jesus Christ.

Thank You for allowing me to live in a country that makes it possible to follow Your divine call on my life. Thank You for instilling in the hearts and minds of our country's forefathers the importance of freedom.

When I consider times past and present, and countries near and far, I count myself blessed to live in the freest country of all. Thank You for allowing me to live in a country that is truly free.

All creation senses a pulsating rhythm deep within to live free. That yearning follows the blueprint of a greater freedom: freedom from the bondage of sin and death, freedom from the law that brings condemnation, freedom to follow Jesus.

Jesus, You laid down Your life to win my freedom. You

have rescued me from the one who rules in the kingdom of darkness. You have purchased my freedom with Your blood and have forgiven all my sins. I rejoice that You have set me free! Sin is no longer my master because I am not under law but under grace.

You have given me a freedom that countries and rulers cannot take away — a freedom I can know even in bondage. "Now the Lord is the Spirit, and where the Spirit of the Lord is, there is freedom." Your Spirit lives in me.

As Americans continue in the footsteps of those who have gone before them, may we experience the freedom that comes from You. May we intuitively know the difference between liberty and license. May we use our freedom to serve one another in love. And may we yield to Jesus Christ, the giver of true freedom.

Scripture references: John 8:36; Romans 6:14, 8:1-3; 2 Corinthians 3:17; Colossians 1:13-14 NLT; 1 Peter 2:16

National Mail Voter Registration

The National Mail Voter Registration Form is the one document that allows you to register to vote from anywhere in the United States. To print the application, visit www.fec.gov/votregis/vr.htm. The National Form can be used to:

1. Register people at your church.
2. Register people at a Bible study or fellowship group.
3. Register family and friends.
4. Register co-workers.

States that accept the national form will accept copies of the application printed from the computer image on regular paper stock, signed by the applicant, and mailed in an envelope with first class postage. In completing this application, be sure to follow the instructions carefully.

> *If the next centennial does not find us a great nation...it will be because those who represent the enterprise, the culture, and the morality of the nation do not aid in controlling the political forces.*
>
> —*James Garfield, 1881*

Prayer 5

Expressing Our Love and Commitment to the One Who Loves Us

"As the Father has loved me, so have I loved you. Now remain in my love. If you obey my commands, you will remain in my love, just as I have obeyed my Father's commands and remain in his love."

John 15:9-10

Almighty God,

Like an avid collector of precious stones, You searched the world far and wide until You found me. I am Your pearl of great price.

Like someone drowning in the middle of the sea, I was helplessly engulfed in the depths of my folly and You saved me. I am the reason You are called Savior.

Like a slave in bondage to a wicked master, I was hopelessly bound in a hell of my own making. Yet You purchased my freedom with Your blood — now I belong to You.

Before I realized I was lost, You found me. Before I knew I was drowning in my narcissistic pursuits, You rescued me. Before I was conscious of my enslavement to sin, You bought me.

Jesus, You demonstrated the full extent of Your love by dying for me — while I was still lost, enslaved, drowning.

Thank You for loving me in my unlovable moments. But even in my strongest moments I must admit that I don't — I can't — hold on to You. You hold on to me. I belong to You, and for that reason I call You Lord.

As I survey the upcoming election, I lay my agenda items aside to seek Your heart. I want Your interests to become my interests. I want Your attitudes to become my attitudes. I want Your ways to become my ways.

I commit myself to You and the furthering of Your kingdom. May You stir within Your people hearts like David's — men and women who pursue the heart of God. Men and women who seek first Your kingdom and Your righteousness.

Please give Your church Your perspective in the upcoming election. May we vote in a way that reflects Your character: Your love, mercy, forgiveness, and a zeal for righteousness. And may we vote in a way that reflects Your heart.

Scripture references: 1 Samuel 13:13; Matthew 6:33; Luke 19:10; Romans 5:8; 1 John 3:16; Revelation 5:9

Offer to drive a shut-in to the polls on November 2

Sadly, millions of Americans are unable to vote because they cannot drive to their polling place, especially disabled people and senior citizens. This is a shame because oftentimes our senior citizens have the most experience in our democratic system. If anyone makes it to the polls, it should be them! Contact your local nursing homes or senior citizen centers and volunteer to drive people to the polls. Some states allow election representatives to go to the voter's home with a paper ballot for the voter to fill in.

The strength of a country is the strength of its religious convictions.
—President Calvin Coolidge, 1921

Prayers for the Election Process

Prayer 6

Moral and Ethical Leadership

These are the last words of David:... "The God of Israel spoke, the Rock of Israel said to me: 'When one rules over men in righteousness, when he rules in the fear of God, he is like the light of morning at sunrise on a cloudless morning, like the brightness after rain that brings the grass from the earth.' "

2 Samuel 23:1,3-4

Almighty God,

Your Word tell us that You love righteousness and hate wickedness, that righteousness exalts a nation and sin is a disgrace to any people. So, Lord, we pray that on November 2, 2004, You would give us elected officials — especially a president — who will lead us into righteousness. Men and women who fear You and hate sin.

Please open our eyes to the candidates who live a congruent lifestyle — people who are the same in private as they are in public. People who are able to identify personal stumbling blocks that lie ahead so they can steer clear of them. Stir within the hearts of the American voters a desire to be led by men and women of character and conscience.

Embed within our leaders a moral anchor that refuses to be moved by any storm of controversy. May they stand on the solid foundation of Your Word, which lasts beyond the fleeting and fashionable definitions our culture gives to morality.

Grant us strong and courageous leaders who are unafraid to take unpopular stands. Give them a sense of Your presence as these men and women of conviction look to You for guidance. May they lead us in a way that touches our hearts so that their moral decisions avoid the appearance of rigid legalism.

Please endow the candidates we elect with humility. Help them to understand that their authority to make decisions comes from You. Give us servant leaders who willingly wash the feet of the American people.

We know that morality doesn't make us a Christian nation, nor is it equivalent to salvation. But, Lord, we pray that You would use the character of our leaders — especially our president — to point the people of our nation to salvation in Jesus Christ.

Scripture references: Joshua 1:9; Psalm 45:7, 116:5; Proverbs 14:34; Matthew 7:24-27, 20:26-28; John 13:14, 19:11

Volunteer to work the polls on Election Day

Voter fraud is a problem in any election. If you're concerned about voter fraud in your precinct, volunteer to work the polls on Election Day. Many people don't know they can volunteer to be a poll worker, and in some states you can even get paid for it. This is a great way to participate in our democracy and will help ensure a fair election. Contact your county government and tell them you want to be a poll worker.

> *Men, in a word, must necessarily be controlled either by a power within them, or a power without them; either by the word of God, or by the strong arm of man; either by the Bible or by the bayonet. It may do for other countries, and other governments to talk about the State supporting religion. Here, under our own free institutions, it is Religion which must support the State.*
>
> *—Robert Winthrop, 1879*

Prayer 7

Balance of Justice and Mercy

He has showed you, O man, what is good. And what does the Lord require of you? To act justly and to love mercy and to walk humbly with your God.

Micah 6:8

Almighty God,

We read in Your Word that You are a God of justice. You are the righteous judge who detests evil and punishes sin. You judge the world in righteousness and the peoples with equity. If anyone turns a deaf ear to the law, even his prayers are detestable to You. And You hold us responsible for the decisions we make.

Yet we also read in Your Word that You are a God of mercy and You delight in showing mercy. You do not treat us as our sins deserve or repay us according to our iniquities. You are "compassionate and gracious, slow to anger, abounding in love." You tell us that if we spend ourselves on behalf of the hungry and satisfy the needs of the oppressed, then our light will rise in the darkness, and our night will become like the noonday.

From our finite mind, the two seem mutually exclusive: How can we pursue both justice and mercy at the same time? Yet You lift them both up as important values of Your kingdom. And if both are a reflection of You and Your ways, how can we make our way through this labyrinth?

Lord, we need elected officials who intuitively know the difference between the two. Give us candidates with an equal love for justice and mercy. Impart to them wisdom so they will know how to apply the two to American life. Stir within the American voters an equal desire for both. What we desire is a country that reflects the values of Your kingdom.

This we do know: we cannot know mercy without justice.

Thank You for sending Jesus to die on the cross to pay the penalty of our sin. May we, Your body of believers, live in the light of this fact.

Scripture references: Psalm 7:11, 31:5; 98:9; 103:8-10; Proverbs 6:10-11, 28:9; Isaiah 58:10; Micah 7:18

Start a grassfire!

Every grassfire starts with a small spark. That was Steve Elliot's theory when he started utilizing breakthrough technology to expand the voices of like-minded citizens on important issues. At www.grassfire.org, you can sign a petition and forward it to your friends and family. You get to see how many friends follow your lead and how many "e-generations" your message travels. You can track your own political "grassfire" and watch it grow! One petition prompted more than 50,000 telephone calls to the office of a prominent United States senator who was soon to vote on pro-life legislation. Think you're just one voice? Think again!

> *God who gave us life gave us liberty. And can the liberties of a nation be thought secure when we have removed their only firm basis, a conviction in the minds of the people that these liberties are of the Gift of God?*
>
> *—Thomas Jefferson, 1780*

Prayer 8

A President After God's Own Heart

"After removing Saul, he made David their king. He testified concerning him: 'I have found David son of Jesse a man after my own heart; he will do everything I want him to do.'"

Acts 13:22

Almighty God,

Your Word tells us, "The eyes of the Lord move to and fro throughout the earth that He may strongly support those whose heart is completely His." You see past our appearance, our education, our occupation, our experience, and You see into our hearts. And those whose hearts are completely Yours find uncommon strength from You.

Lord, as we enter into the upcoming presidential election, we ask that You would give us a president who is a man after Your own heart.

Give us a president who will shepherd us with integrity and truth. May he be a man who places the American people above himself. May he be a man of conviction who is more concerned about doing what is right than he is about securing a high approval rating.

Guide us to the candidate who is able to maintain a semblance of innocence in the midst of what is often a jaded political process. Although no one is perfect, show us which candidate has been tainted the least and who desires what is best for all Americans.

Please lead us to a man who not only has deep-seated morals but is grounded in a relationship with You. May he seek direction from Your Word and from godly advisors. May he be a man of prayer who doesn't usurp Your authority but understands that he is answerable to You. And may he be a man courageous enough to walk in obedience to what You have required of Him.

Equip our president with the skills to lead the American people with knowledge and understanding. Give Him the wisdom to know how to bring the American people along with him as He follows after You.

Lord God, You are the one who sets up kings and deposes them. You are the one who gives wisdom to the wise and knowledge to the discerning. On November 4, open the eyes of the American voters so we will see past the appearances and into the heart. Through our president, may You turn our hearts toward You.

Scripture references: 1 Samuel 13:14, 16:7; 1 Kings 8:58; 2 Chronicles 16:9 (NASB95); Psalm 78:72; Isaiah 3:16; Jeremiah 3:15; Daniel 2:21

Attend your local caucus or precinct meetings

The United States of America is divided into geographic precincts. A precinct is usually the size of a large neighborhood. Long before you see the large conventions on television, smaller groups meet in local precinct (sometimes called caucus) meetings. These neighborhood groups are an extremely crucial part of the political process. This is where delegates to county conventions — and eventually to the national convention — are selected. This is also where each political party decides what they stand for and against in their party platforms. For information, contact your local Republican or Democratic party headquarters.

Men who see not God in our history have surely lost sight of the fact that, from the landing of the Mayflower to this hour, the great men whose names are indissolubly associated with the colonization, rise, and progress of the Republic have borne testimony to the vital truths of Christianity.

—Henry Wilson, 1873

Prayer 9

Discerning Leaders

The Lord was pleased that Solomon had asked for this. So God said to him, "Since you have asked for this and not for long life or wealth for yourself, nor have asked for the death of your enemies but for discernment in administering justice, I will do what you have asked. I will give you a wise and discerning heart, so that there will never have been anyone like you, nor will there ever be. Moreover, I will give you what you have not asked for—both riches and honor—so that in your lifetime you will have no equal among kings.

1 Kings 3:10-13

Almighty God,

Leading a nation is a sobering responsibility because the needs of the many exist at the mercy of the few. The siren call of power can easily seduce leaders into making disastrous decisions that disintegrate families, tear societies apart, and, in the end, set nations in opposition to You.

Lord, You are the giver of all wisdom, and from Your mouth comes knowledge and understanding. Please give us decisive leaders who have the wisdom that comes from heaven. Wisdom that is pure, peace-loving, considerate, submissive, full of mercy and good fruit, impartial, and sincere.

Your Word tells us, "Without wise leadership, a nation falls; with many counselors, there is safety." Endow our new leaders with humility so they will acknowledge their own shortcomings and their need for wise counsel. Surround them with men and women of wisdom and discernment, and give them the foresight to rely on godly spiritual leaders as well.

On November 2, 2004, lead the American voters to candidates with discerning hearts who not only know how to distinguish right from wrong, but are committed to upholding and enforcing what is good and what is right. We ask that You would give us discerning leaders who intuitively know when they are standing at the threshold of deception and are unafraid to back away.

For this reason, Lord, we need leaders with wisdom *and* discernment. Leaders able to discern the real needs of the American people and wise enough to know how to bring us with them through often uncertain waters.

May the foremost concern of our incoming leaders not be political success or the wealth of this country or victory over our enemies, but may it be the governing of the American people with wisdom and discernment.

Scripture references: Proverbs 2:6, 11:14 (NLT); Romans 16:27; James 3:17

Start a petition, go door-to-door

Petitions work! In 2003, the citizens of California petitioned their governor out of office. Gray Davis had been regarded as one of the more socially liberal and homosexual-friendly governors in America. When Darrel Issa started a petition to recall the governor, more than 1 million Californians signed on to force him out of office. You don't need permission to start a petition, but you should check with local election offices as there may be special rules and procedures you need to follow.

Religion and virtue are the only foundations, not only of republicanism and of all free government, but of social felicity under all governments and in all the combinations of human society. Our Constitution was made only for a moral and religious people. It is wholly inadequate to the government of any other.

—John Adams, 1811

Prayer 10

Discerning Voters

Then Elihu said: "Listen to me, you wise men. Pay attention, you who have knowledge. 'Just as the mouth tastes good food, the ear tests the words it hears.' So let us discern for ourselves what is right; let us learn together what is good."

Job 34:1-4 (NLT)

Almighty God,

During election time we, the voting public, are bombarded with messages and promises — many which sound reasonable and truthful. But we're soon thrown into confusion when we hear contradicting messages and promises of others which also sound reasonable and truthful. Unfortunately the claim that broadcasts the clearest and loudest is often victorious — even if it doesn't reflect Your will and Your ways.

Jesus, we need ears to hear through the cacophony of claims that solicit our vote. Because You are truth, we look to You to steer us through this confusion. By Your Spirit of truth, guide us through the messages of every candidate and issue. Please expose any hype or fraudulent claims that may lead us astray from Your truth.

You tell us in Your Word,

> *Let those who are wise understand these things. Let those who are discerning listen carefully. The paths of the Lord are true and right, and righteous people live by walking in them. But sinners stumble and fall along the way.*
>
> *Hosea 14:9 NLT*

Your paths are true and right, and righteous people live by walking in them. Give us eyes to see the paths of righteousness which lie before us. Make us aware of the stumbling blocks that lie hidden along the way. May we not judge by mere appearances but make the right judgment. Most of all, transform our nation so we will become a righteous people.

You have made Your truth evident to everyone, and Your wrath is vented against those who suppress it. We have no excuse for ignoring Your truth. Please open our eyes to the bondage that comes from self-deception.

Your truth brings freedom — stir within the American people a love for truth that frees us from our meaningless self-pursuits that ultimately lead to death. And grant us the courage to make the difficult decisions that lead to life. We need a greater vision that transcends ourselves. A vision that leads us to You.

Scripture references: Hosea 14:9 (NLT); John 7:24, 8:32, 14:6; Romans 1:18-19; 2 Thessalonians 2:9-11

Give away copies of *We Will Pray for Election Day*

We're concerned about the plight of America today, and we need your help to get this book into the hands of millions of voters. Will you join this movement? To order copies of this book, visit www.TheChristianVote.org. We give discounts to churches and civic organizations. You can also download sermon notes on our website to use for informing your congregation about the elections.

> *We have staked the whole future of American civilization, not upon the power of government, far from it. We have staked the future of all of our political institutions upon the capacity of mankind for self-government; upon the capacity of each and all of us to govern ourselves, to control ourselves, to sustain ourselves according to the Ten Commandments of God.*
>
> *—James Madison, 1778*

Prayer 11

A Church That Models Jesus

We love because he first loved us. If anyone says, "I love God," yet hates his brother, he is a liar. For anyone who does not love his brother, whom he has seen, cannot love God, whom he has not seen. And he has given us this command: Whoever loves God must also love his brother.

1 John 4:19-21

Almighty God,

The greatest indicator of Your presence among us, Your church, is not our inspiring words or our stand for truth or our holy lives. It's love.

Jesus, we need Your love to permeate Your people during this election: our words, our stand for truth, our lives. May the fruit of Your Spirit flow through us in everything we do — Your love, joy, peace, patience, kindness, goodness, faithfulness, gentleness, and self-control.

Please help us to love our fellow Americans well — even those who oppose us and seemingly oppose the truth of Your Word. If we are falsely accused, give us the strength to refrain from striking back just as You refrained from striking back when You stood silent before Your accusers. *More important than being right is loving as You have loved us.*

Silence the voices of those who claim to know You but prove otherwise by their actions. May we be slow in our rush to judgment regarding the private lives of our candidates, knowing that all of us stand on feet of clay. Give us eyes to see that those who disagree with us are more than mere labels. And give us Your wisdom to know when we are hurting the cause of the gospel and when we are working with You to proclaim it.

At the same time, please place Your words in our mouths. Words that speak the truth in love. Words that speak prophetically to our nation. And, most of all, words that lift up Your name and draw our nation to You.

The potential power we Christians wield as a voting bloc is seductive and deadly. Please work in us so that our goal is not control but transformation of the human heart, where real change takes place. Through our unity may the world know that You came to save us from ourselves.

Jesus, You prayed to Your heavenly Father, "My prayer is not that you take them out of the world but that you protect them from the evil one." Please show us how we can engage the world according to Your prayer as You protect us from the evil one.

During this election our desire is that we would live such good lives among those who don't know You that they will be drawn to You and Your truth. Through our actions may people glimpse Your beauty, Your holiness, and Your love. Through us may people see Jesus.

Scripture references: Mark 15:3-5; John 12:32, 17:15, 20-23; Galatians 5:22-23; Ephesians 4:15; 1 Peter 2:12; 1 John 4:19

Write a letter to the editor

Newspapers in this country seldom include news articles from a Christian viewpoint, but they will publish a letter to the editor. Since the "opinion" section is often the most read page of a newspaper, here is an opportunity for you to make a difference. Write a letter to your editor sharing your views on an important issue or to support a political candidate. Be clear and concise, brief and to the point, and try to keep your letter to fewer than 250 words. If your letter gets published, make copies to distribute in your neighborhood or to friends and family.

Those people who will not be governed by God will be ruled by tyrants.

—William Penn, 1722

Prayer 12

Protection From Harm

God is our refuge and strength, an ever-present help in trouble. Therefore we will not fear, though the earth give way and the mountains fall into the heart of the sea, though its waters roar and foam and the mountains quake with their surging.

Psalm 46:1-3

Almighty God,

What hope would we have if You weren't Lord of heaven and earth? Thank You that Your dominion extends over every inch of soil and every person, thought, and plan. The earth is Yours and everything in it, the world, and all who live in it.

For this reason we come before You to seek Your protection and peace during the election. "You are my hiding place; you will protect me from trouble and surround me with songs of deliverance."

As we proceed through the election campaigns, primaries, conventions, and Election Day on November 2, 2004, we ask that You would thwart the plans of those who intend to disrupt or undermine our system of government. Please place a hedge of protection around our candidates and foil any attempts by individuals who seek to assassinate them.

Dispatch Your angels to our country's borders and prevent any outsiders from entering whose intent is our destruction. We ask that You would expose any terrorist plots against people, monuments, or cities. Protect the American people from bioterrorist, chemical, or nuclear threats.

At the same time we ask that You would open the eyes of the men and women who serve under our Office of Homeland Security so they will be able to identify any present or future danger to our country. Please orchestrate events so that those who work in intelligence will uncover every insidious plot. Grant discernment to those who work in immigration so they will intuitively know who to prevent from entering our country. And coordinate the communication in and between our regional governments and federal governmental agencies so they will effectively share the information that is received.

Yet we know we can't run anywhere to be completely safe from harm. But we can run to You. Your name is a strong tower. The righteous run to it and are safe. You are our refuge and strength, an ever-present help in trouble.

May the threats we face draw our attention to the reality of eternity. Please use our present situation to draw our hearts to You and seek Your salvation through Jesus Christ.

Scripture references: Job 1:10; Psalm 11:1, 24:1, 32:7, 46:1; Proverbs 18:10; Acts 17:24

Read and distribute political scorecards

One way to research a candidate's views or voting record is with a political scorecard. What's a political scorecard? Organizations compile and compare the views and voting records of candidates and then make them available as printed scorecards. There are literally hundreds of scorecards, but the most prominent of them are the liberal Americans for Democratic Action (www.adaction.org) and the conservative American Conservative Union (www.acuratings.com) scorecard. You can also develop your own political scorecard of local candidates. Make a questionnaire of issues and ask local candidates to record their views, then share this information with others.

I have carefully examined the evidences of the Christian religion, and if I was sitting as a juror upon its authenticity I would unhesitatingly give my verdict in its favor. I can prove its truth as clearly as any proposition ever submitted to the mind of man.

—Alexander Hamilton, 1802

Prayer 13

Campaigns Grounded in Truth

These are the things you are to do: Speak the truth to each other, and render true and sound judgment in your courts; do not plot evil against your neighbor, and do not love to swear falsely.

Zechariah 8:16-17

Almighty God,

All of us wrestle with the temptation to make ourselves appear better than we really are: To tell people what they want to hear. To make promises we know we cannot keep. To point out the faults in others over the faults of our own. And, in reality, election campaigns only reflect what lies in every heart.

But You are the God who sees all, the God who knows us better than we know ourselves. You aren't impressed with our words, credentials, or experience because You look at our hearts.

Your Word tells us that out of the abundance of the heart the mouth speaks. Please reveal what resides within the candidates' hearts. Bring clarity to their words and help them avoid the doublespeak which only causes ambiguity and confusion.

We read in Your Word that You detest lying lips, but You delight in those who are truthful. God, as we sift through the endless claims and promises in the upcoming election, please move the campaign officials and marketing directors to address the public with truth.

Stifle the hype that suppresses what is real and focus our campaigns on facts rather than falsehood. Please muffle the voices that distort truth and proclaim false accusation. Shut the mouths that utter slander and malice. Show us that when we point our finger at others, we often fail to see our own shortcomings.

Please enlighten our political candidates to the folly of making promises based on the shaky ground of polls and surveys. We need leaders who are unafraid to take clear stands on vague issues. We need leaders who stand on the solid ground of truth and who value character and honesty.

"Words of wisdom come from the wise, but fools speak foolishness." May You use the words of our candidates and referendums to reveal the extent of Your wisdom or our foolishness.

Scripture references: 1 Samuel 16:7; Psalm 7:9; Proverbs 12:22, 15:2 (CEV); Matthew 12:34

Join a club or organization

Most communities have a variety of political clubs and organizations you can join. Some of them are issue-oriented while others are citizen organizations that focus on voter registration. Some of the larger organizations are Eagle Forum, Concerned Women of America, 60 Plus, and American Life League. These organizations are influential, especially in national elections. You can join, attend meetings, and become active in their causes.

> *The Bible is one of the greatest blessings bestowed by God on the children of men. It has God for its author; salvation for its end, and truth without any mixture for its matter. It is all pure, all sincere; nothing too much; nothing wanting.*
>
> *—John Locke, 1698*

Prayer 14

Fair and Balanced Media

"Here is your part: Tell the truth. Be fair. Live at peace with everyone. Don't plot harm to others; don't swear that something is true when it isn't! How I hate all that sort of thing!" says the Lord.

Zechariah 8:16-17 TLB

Almighty God,

During an election a great deal of the information we rely on to make decisions regarding candidates and issues comes from the media. We are at their mercy when getting our news. And because the media is composed of subjective people like me, I know that I cannot expect completely objective reporting.

Despite this fact, the media can be a vehicle that dispenses truth. Please set a guard over the voices of our newspapers, radio stations, and television networks. We ask that You prevent any unwholesome talk from coming out of our news outlets except what is helpful for building others up, that it may benefit all of us who listen.

Stir within our media an insatiable hunger for truth. We ask that You would reveal Your truth about the candidates and issues through the media and that they would become purveyors of Your truth without even realizing it.

Increase within them a distaste for half-truths, hype, libel, exaggeration, and bias. Your Word tells us that You detest lying lips, but You delight in men who are truthful. Close their ears to the false accusations and lies that often denigrate people and issues in elections so that only truth is communicated.

In an age of sound bites and talking heads, may they model to the American people integrity, impartiality, and fairness. May they show no favoritism just as You show no favoritism. May they focus on what is important: issues and character.

Despite living in an increasingly secular society, which the media increasingly parallels, we also understand that the media are not the enemy. We fight a much greater enemy: the devil, who hates truth and is the father of lies. Lord, we ask that You would shut the mouth of the enemy so that he has no influence in the coming election.

Thank You Jesus for being the embodiment of truth. You are the way, the truth, and the life. May the media's pursuit of truth become an unknowing pursuit of You. Use them to reveal the nauseating folly of excess and the bankruptcy of lives lived apart from You. But most of all, may You use them to reveal Yourself.

Scripture references: Psalm 141:3; Proverbs 12:22; John 8:44, 14:6; Acts 10:34; Ephesians 4:29; 1 Timothy 5:21

Support Israel

Today in the news, we hear a lot about Israel and problems in the Middle East. The Bible says, "Pray for the peace of Jerusalem, they shall prosper that love thee" (Psalm 122:6). As Christians, we ought to support and pray for the Jewish people and for peace in the Middle East. Christians owe a debt of eternal gratitude to the Jewish people for their contributions that gave birth to the Christian faith. Jesus said, "Salvation is of the Jews!" (John 4:22). To get involved in the support of Israel, and to help Jews around the world through Operation Exodus, contact John Hagee Ministries at 800-854-9899.

It cannot be emphasized too strongly or too often that this great nation was founded, not by religionists, but by Christians; not on religions, but on the gospel of Jesus Christ. For this very reason peoples of other faiths have been afforded asylum, prosperity, and freedom of worship here.

—Patrick Henry, 1775

Prayer 15

Honest Elections

So when the crowd had gathered, Pilate asked them, "Which one do you want me to release to you: Barabbas, or Jesus who is called Christ?" For he knew it was out of envy that they had handed Jesus over to him. While Pilate was sitting on the judge's seat, his wife sent him this message: "Don't have anything to do with that innocent man, for I have suffered a great deal today in a dream because of him." But the chief priests and the elders persuaded the crowd to ask for Barabbas and to have Jesus executed.

Matthew 27:17-20

Almighty God,

We read throughout Your Word that You defend the poor and oppressed. You are above bribery and You value the integrity of a person's word. You love honesty and detest corruption. You abhor dishonest scales — they are an abomination to You — but accurate weights are Your delight.

Although democracy isn't mentioned directly in Scripture, honesty is. In the coming election we ask that You would guard the integrity of our decisions. From the voters to the people who count our ballots, we ask that You would secure the voting process.

Safeguard any unsuspecting people against voting out of coercion or obligation to another person or group. Holy Spirit, we invite You to convict and prevent anyone from casting a vote that doesn't rightfully belong to them. Because You are a God of justice, our desire is that race, age, gender, education, and income will not be a factor in who votes on November 2.

Please give our governmental authorities keen eyes and discerning minds to detect voter fraud. Alert them to irregularities in our electronic voting systems and abnormalities in the way ballots are counted. We ask for You to place men and women impervious to corruption at our polling places to ensure that our votes aren't compromised.

Grant wisdom to any judges who may have to render verdicts that determine what constitutes a valid vote or the legality of an election. May they balance the scales of justice with equity, integrity, and impartiality.

Although honest elections preserve the fidelity of our democracy, we refuse to place our trust in the voting process. We place our hope in You knowing that You are the One who weeds out corruption and the One who ensures that honesty guides our election.

Scripture references: Deuteronomy 10:17; Psalm 25:21, 82:3-4; Proverbs 11:1,3; Isaiah 30:18; Amos 5:12; Matthew 5:37

March in a parade

Getting involved in a political campaign can be fun for the whole family! Contact a local candidate (a candidate you feel good about supporting) and volunteer to march in parades on his or her behalf. Most candidates participate in dozens of local parades during the campaign. You can ride along with a candidate, march along with a banner, or walk along the curbsides passing out campaign literature. You'll probably get a free T-shirt for your work, and your family will have a blast!

America was born a Christian nation. America was born to exemplify that devotion to the elements of righteousness, which are derived from the revelations of Holy Scriptures. Part of the destiny of Americans lies in their daily perusal of this great book of revelations. That if they would see America free and pure they will make their own spirits free and pure by this baptism of the Holy Spirit.

—President Woodrow Wilson, 1934

Prayer 16

High Voter Turnout

A proclamation was then issued throughout Judah and Jerusalem for all the exiles to assemble in Jerusalem. Anyone who failed to appear within three days would forfeit all his property, in accordance with the decision of the officials and elders, and would himself be expelled from the assembly of the exiles.

Ezra 10:7-8

Almighty God,

As we approach November 2, we ask that You would stir the hearts of the American people.

Awaken us from our complacency so we will take the upcoming election seriously and vote. May we witness an extraordinary turnout at the polls so that the candidates elected and issues passed will truly represent the American people and not special interests.

Pull us out of our individualistic mindset that assumes every person is autonomous. And build within our nation a sense of community so that everyone will see that they are playing a part in the decision-making process through the candidates we elect and the issues we approve.

All too often, we lose heart in the election process because we believe our vote won't make a difference. Remind us of the 2000 Presidential Election when every vote *did* count. May we not regret in the future our complacencies of the past.

All too often we also lose heart because we feel that regardless of the candidate, status quo will continue. For this reason we ask that You will give us candidates who will inspire us to vote. May they be men and women of overwhelming integrity, a clear sense of vision, and the ability to move us to higher ideals which reflect biblical values. Please give us candidates who will walk their talk and fulfill their promises.

On Election Day we ask that You would grant us good

weather throughout our nation so that people wouldn't be discouraged from voting. Give the American people generous hearts so that we will be willing to transport men and women to the polls who wouldn't be able to transport themselves.

Last of all, renew our confidence in the election process. Please remind us that You can take the chaos of Election Day to assert Your will. For this reason we refuse to place our trust in the election. We place our trust in You.

Scripture references: Judges 21:5-6; Amos 6:1; 1 Corinthians 1:10

Get out the vote

Usually the candidate who wins an election is the one who gets the most supporters to the polls. If an election is close, it all comes down to voter turnout. You can help your favorite candidates by getting out the vote on Election Day. How? Most campaigns have lists of supporters with telephone numbers and e-mail addresses. Volunteer to help contact these voters to remind them to vote. Because we are all so busy, sometimes we forget.

> *Of all the dispositions and habits which lead to political prosperity, religion and morality are indispensable supports. Let us with caution indulge the supposition that morality can be maintained without religion. Whatever may be conceded to the influence of refined education on minds of peculiar structure, reason and experience both forbid us to expect that national morality can prevail in exclusion of religious principle.*
>
> *—President George Washington, 1796*

Prayer 17

Order on Election Day

Obey the government, for God is the one who put it there. All governments have been placed in power by God. So those who refuse to obey the laws of the land are refusing to obey God, and punishment will follow.

Romans 13:1-2 NLT

Submit yourselves for the Lord's sake to every human institution, whether to a king as the one in authority, or to governors as sent by him for the punishment of evildoers and the praise of those who do right.

1 Peter 2:13-14 NASB95

Almighty God,

Thank You for allowing me to live in a country where I have the opportunity to cast my vote for people and issues according to my convictions. May You enact Your will through the American voters.

At the same time, we know that an enemy lurks who seeks to undermine the election. On November 2, we ask that You would prevent any terrorist attack — foreign or American — from harming our country. Protect our candidates, our cities, our monuments, our borders, our troops from anything and anyone who would seek to adversely influence the election or strike fear in the hearts of our voters.

We pray for honest elections at the polls. May polling workers, vote counters, government workers, and party officials guard the integrity of the election. We ask that You would uncover voter fraud, even if it benefits our candidates and issues.

Regardless of the outcome, help the American people to accept the candidate who is elected. If issues are passed that depart from the convictions of Your people, give us wisdom to know how to follow due process to see those issues overturned.

Remind us to be subject to rulers and authorities, to be obedient, to be ready to do whatever is good. In the event that conflict or confusion arises regarding the results, please help us to seek peace and pursue it. And give us an insatiable desire for truth so that justice will prevail.

Lord, You have set up our system of government. We submit to it and desire to treat it with respect out of deference to You. For this reason we ask that You would preserve and maintain order in the United States on November 2.

Scripture references: Romans 13:1-2; Titus 3:1; 1 Peter 2:13-14, 3:11, 5:8

What is a Political Action Committee (PAC)?

Special interest groups form Political Action Committees (PACs) so they can contribute to candidates and parties. When many small contributions are pooled together, they can be substantial enough to make a difference. PACs are formed by corporations, unions, or by groups of people who feel strongly about issues. One of the most prominent PACs started by Christians is the Campaign for Working Families (CWF), which is dedicated to electing pro-family, pro-life and pro-free enterprise candidates. CWF has raised more than $7 million to become one of the largest PACs in the country. For information, contact CWF at (703) 671-8800 or visit www.campaignforfamilies.org. You can also start your own PAC with friends who share a similar view on an issue. Call 1-800-424-9530 for information.

Only a virtuous people are capable of freedom. As nations become corrupt and vicious, they have more need of masters.
—Benjamin Franklin, 1773

Prayers for Issues

Prayer 18

Sanctity of Human Life: The Unborn

For you created my inmost being; you knit me together in my mother's womb. I praise you because I am fearfully and wonderfully made; your works are wonderful, I know that full well. My frame was not hidden from you when I was made in the secret place. When I was woven together in the depths of the earth, your eyes saw my unformed body. All the days ordained for me were written in your book before one of them came to be.

Psalm 139:13-16

Almighty God,

The miracle of human life is beyond comprehension! How could You know me and love me before You even formed me in my mother's womb? Why would You choose to create me in Your image when You knew I would fall woefully short of Your holiness?

You valued me so much that You paid for my sin with the blood of Your Son Jesus. How wide and long and high and deep is Your great love, which is embodied in Christ.

Heavenly Father, Your heart must break over the way we treat those whom You labored to create in Your image. Please forgive our nation for regarding human life as dispensable, disposable, and cheap. Forgive us for mortgaging the lives of the unborn in order to safeguard the conveniences of the present. By suppressing the truth, we are invoking Your wrath.

Through the coming election we ask that You would bring to the leadership of our nation men and women of conscience. Men and women who fear You more than the prevailing opinions of our day, who understand that abortion is tantamount to murder.

Please give us leaders who will articulate their pro-life position clearly and convincingly while avoiding condemnation. Help them to speak the truth in love so that those who oppose them will listen because they don't feel backed into a corner. Give them wisdom to offer solutions to this issue that show compassion for both the mother and child, and especially for the poor.

At the same time please prevent any protesters from undermining our cause through murder and violence. Let the world see that the pro-life movement is truly pro-life — whether born or unborn.

Lord God, please move in the hearts of the American people so they will understand that life is sacred and the right to take someone's life only belongs to You. Help our nation to see that by allowing abortion to continue we are really hurting ourselves: we're hardening our hearts toward You, we're destroying our ability to love, and we're heaping guilt upon ourselves that suffocates our souls.

Open our eyes to see that the abortion issue is a window into our hearts. Please renew our commitment to the sanctity of human life, and draw us to the author of life — Jesus Christ.

Scripture references: Genesis 1:27; Psalm 139:13-16; Acts 3:15; Romans 1:18; Ephesians 3:18

Answer telephone surveys

From time to time you may receive a telephone call from a pollster. We are all bothered by telemarketers, but if you want your voice to be heard you should politely listen and give your honest feedback. Why? Most polls are samplings of a very small population, so even though you are only one person, your answers could have nationwide impact. While your vote is one of millions, your answer to a poll may be one of only hundreds. These polls are often touted by candidates and in the news media to sway voters.

The safest road to Hell is the gradual one—the gentle slope, soft underfoot, without sudden turnings, without milestones, without signposts.

—C.S. Lewis, 1961

Prayer 19

Sanctity of Human Life: A Culture of Violence

The commandments, "Do not commit adultery," "Do not murder," "Do not steal," "Do not covet," and whatever other commandment there may be, are summed up in this one rule: "Love your neighbor as yourself." Love does no harm to its neighbor. Therefore love is the fulfillment of the law.

Romans 13:9-10

Almighty God,

Thousands of years ago You destroyed all the people on earth with a flood — except for Noah and his family — because the earth was filled with violence. Then You promised to never destroy us again with a flood. Thank You for not punishing us according to our sins as we deserve.

Yet through this example and others in Scripture we know that violence is not pleasing to You. Forgive us for profaning — making common — the miracle of life You have given to us.

On November 2, 2004, please guide the American voters to candidates who are committed to curtailing our culture of violence. Candidates who sincerely value the sanctity of human life. Candidates who are committed to forging a culture of nonviolence, peace, and respect. Please give these candidates wisdom to know how to restrain our culture without being legalistic or heavy-handed.

At the same time, work within the hearts of the American people. Open our eyes to the adverse effects of the violence glorified in the movies and television shows we watch, the music we listen to, and the video games we play. We have eaten the food of wickedness and drunk from the cup of violence. Now, by Your Holy Spirit, make all of this nauseating to us.

We need You to breathe new life into our numbed hearts. Move within our parents so they will actively involve themselves in their children's lives. Help our parents and political candidates to realize that the solution to gangs and school violence resides not in stiffer laws but rather in active parenting.

All too often we barter the dignity of others to satisfy our own lusts. Forgive us for allowing a sexualized culture to flourish which views women as a commodity and sex as merely an innocuous activity. Through the upcoming election, bring to our leadership men and women who understand that pornography degrades men and women in a passively violent way. Guide our newly elected candidates toward creating healthier restraints on our culture.

Lord Jesus, stemming the tide of violence in our country seems overwhelming. We know that even the healthiest restraints and the most effective legislation are not enough. You are the only solution to our myriad problems. Through Your death on the cross, You reconciled us to God and brought an end to our hostilities. Please bring to our nation the peace that comes from knowing You.

Scripture references: Genesis 6:13, 9:15; Proverbs 4:17; Ephesians 2:16

Stand In the Gap For the Unborn

Over the last 30 years, more than 40 million unborn babies have been killed at the hands of abortionists. Help support key pro-life initiatives that include bans on cloning, research that destroys human embryos, the RU-486 abortion drug, and taxpayer support of Planned Parenthood (an organization that performed 227,385 abortions last year while referring only 1,963 women to adoption services). If you want to help, contact the National Right to Life (NRLC) at 202-626-8800, or visit www.nrlc.com.

There is not a truth to be gathered form history more certain, or more momentous, than this: that civil liberty cannot long be separated from religious liberty without danger, and ultimately without destruction to both. Wherever religious liberty exists, it will, first or last, bring in and establish political liberty.

—Benjamin Rush, 1788

Prayer 20

Preservation of the Family

For this reason a man will leave his father and mother and be united to his wife, and they will become one flesh.

Genesis 2:24

Children are a gift from the Lord; they are a reward from him.

Psalm 127:3 NLT

Almighty God,

Never before in our nation's history has the family faced an assault on every side like it does right now. Without Your intervention, the family as You ordained it has little hope.

In the remaining time leading up to November 2, 2004, we ask that You would stir the hearts of the American people and the candidates who are running for office. Move us away from the unbiblical definitions of what constitutes a family. Instead, lead us to Your objective definition of the family based upon the solid foundation of Your Word.

From the very beginning, You ordained that man and woman would be joined together to become one flesh. And this one-flesh relationship would be preserved by a marriage covenant. Yet our nation is thrown into confusion by the blessing of gay unions and the countless unmarried couples who live together. Lord, bring us back to our senses and bring us back to Your original design.

Divorce has become an acceptable reality in our society — both in the church and outside the church. Please cover our marriages and protect them from attack and our own flesh-craving tendencies. Give us the strength to persevere and build strong marriages based on love and an ardent dependence upon You.

Convict our parents when they pursue their self-fulfillment and pleasures at the cost of the well-being of their children. Please steer our nation in such a way that our children will grow up in homes where they are raised by their married birth parents in an atmosphere of love and acceptance.

We pray for those children who are growing up in single-parent families. May You fill the void of the missing parent in their lives and use it to bring them to the saving knowledge of Jesus Christ. Help them to realize that they aren't inferior to other children because they didn't grow up with both parents. And heal the damage that might prevent them from forming intimate relationships in the future.

Heavenly Father, we need courageous men and women candidates who will defend the family. Encourage them when they feel criticized and belittled during this election. Give them anointed answers when they are questioned regarding their stand. Please work through them so that Your definition of a family again becomes a priority for our nation.

Thank You that because we have You we are never without hope. Move in the hearts of the American voters so that the family as You designed it is preserved.

Scripture references: Genesis 2:20-24; Psalm 10:14; Lamentations 3:21-22; Malachi 2:14, 2:16

Research the issues

Before you jump into helping a candidate or a cause, you should research the issues. But with so much information available, where do you start? Founded in 1973, the Heritage Foundation is a research and educational institute whose mission is to formulate and promote public policies based on the principles of our Founding Fathers. Their expert staff can help give you the tools you need to research the issues. To contact the Heritage Foundation, write 214 Massachusetts Ave. NE, Washington, DC 20002-4999, 202-546-4400, or visit www.heritage.org.

"It is impossible to mentally or socially enslave a Bible-reading people."
— Horace Greeley, 1852

Prayer 21

Our Older Americans

Rise in the presence of the aged, show respect for the elderly and revere your God. I am the Lord.

Leviticus 19:32

Almighty God,

You are the Ancient of Days, the Alpha and Omega, the beginning and the end. Long before You created us, You were there. We love You because You first loved us, and our act of loving You is merely a response to Your initial actions toward us.

In the same way we remember the aged, those who walk a few steps ahead of us, who cared for us when we couldn't care for ourselves, who provided for us when we couldn't provide for ourselves. Open our hearts and minds to the plight of our older Americans so they aren't ignored during the twilight years of their lives.

In the fifth commandment You tell us to honor our father and mother, and You conclude it with a promise: "that it may go well with you and that you may enjoy long life on the earth." May we not miss Your blessing because we failed to adequately honor our parents — especially when they needed us.

Please draw the American voters to candidates in the upcoming election who are sincerely concerned about the welfare of our senior citizens. Give these men and women wisdom to know how to supply adequate healthcare amidst the skyrocketing cost of medicine. Help our leaders sort through the tangled mess of pharmaceutical coverage so that every older American has adequate means to the medication he or she needs.

In the coming years we will need a plan to ensure that our

taxes pay for an increasing number of seniors within a decreasing taxpayer base. Please develop a plan through our political leaders that is larger than party politics and special interest groups.

With all of this in mind, inspire us to generously share with those who helped create the wealth our nation enjoys. And let it begin with Your church. You tell us in Your Word, "If anyone does not provide for his relatives, and especially for his immediate family, he has denied the faith and is worse than an unbeliever." Give us creative ideas to provide for those in the household of faith and for those in our communities — apart from governmental intervention. May You model Your love to the world through the church's example in society.

Scripture references: Ezra 7:27; Daniel 7:9; Ephesians 6:2-3; 1 Timothy 5:4,8; 1 John 4:19; Revelation 1:8, 21:6

Become a yard-sign coordinator

A campaign manager would be very impressed if you volunteered to be a yard-sign coordinator for your neighborhood. Yard signs can make a big difference because many voters make their decisions based on popularity and name-recognition rather than the issues. Contact the candidates of your choice and tell them you want to place 25, 50, or 100 yard signs in your area. They are free, of course, and you'll have fun making a difference in your neighborhood.

We all can pray. We all should pray. We should ask the fulfillment of God's will. We should ask for courage, wisdom, for the quietness of soul which comes alone to them who place their lives in His hands.

—President Harry S. Truman, 1956

Prayer 22

Morality in Our Culture

Everyone must submit himself to the governing authorities, for there is no authority except that which God has established. The authorities that exist have been established by God. For rulers hold no terror for those who do right, but for those who do wrong. Do you want to be free from fear of the one in authority? Then do what is right and he will commend you. For he is God's servant to do you good.

Romans 13:1, 3-4a

Almighty God,

Thank You that when our country was formed two centuries ago, You gave us founding fathers who believed in right and wrong. And although they weren't perfect, they understood the importance of a moral foundation based on the bedrock of Scripture and a belief in God.

Your Word tells us that righteousness exalts a nation and sin is a disgrace to any people. Undoubtedly, the greatness of our nation has been undergirded by the moral anchors You have supplied us — anchors that have secured us through countless storms of spiritual indifference and moral turpitude.

God, at this time in our nation's history we need You to drive those moral anchors deeper. Keep us steadfast amidst the winds of amorality and immorality. Stir the hearts of the American people so they will know that You are the one true God, the God of righteousness and justice, the God who alone defines sin.

Forgive us for granting our sinful natures the license to run rampant. We have exchanged the truth of God for a lie, and worshipped and served created things rather than the Creator. Please renew within us the belief in absolutes that transcend individual preference. Redirect our priorities toward whatever is true, noble, right, pure, lovely, admirable, excellent, and praiseworthy.

Please bring to our leadership through the upcoming election men and women of virtue who value modesty over immodesty, purity over impurity, respect over tolerance, and integrity over corruption. Give us leaders who understand that the role of government is to punish those who do wrong and praise those who do right. Give us leaders endowed with the wisdom to know how to restrain sin without unduly controlling the American people.

It's no surprise that our country's moral tethers have deteriorated. Apart from Christ, our flesh is stronger than our good intentions. We know that a moral life can never be equated with trusting in Your Son Jesus for our salvation. But may our hunger for morality lead to Christ and may our resulting morality be a response to what Christ has done for us. And in the end, may we find ourselves standing on the solid foundation of the Word made flesh. "For no one can lay any foundation other than the one already laid, which is Jesus Christ."

Scripture references: Proverbs 14:34; Isaiah 30:18, 45:21; John 17:25; Romans 1:25; 1 Corinthians 3:11; Philippians 4:8; 1 Peter 2:14

Donate money to a political campaign

Running a campaign is expensive. The costs to do direct mail, print yard signs, and produce and run advertisements can run thousands of dollars, even for small local elections. You may be surprised to learn that most of the money raised by candidates is in small amounts: $25, $50, or $100. One recent candidate for president raised millions of dollars, all in small amounts. So you don't have to be rich to make a difference. Choose your favorite candidate and make a small contribution. If you want to make a contribution but aren't sure which candidate, to support, contact the Madison Project at (703) 730-6262, or visit www.MadisonProject.org.

> *Let us pray for ourselves, that we may not lose the word "concern" out of our Christian vocabulary. Let us pray for our nation. Let us pray for those who have never known Jesus Christ and redeeming love, for moral forces everywhere, for our national leaders. Let prayer be our passion. Let prayer be our practice.*
>
> *—Robert E. Lee, 1864*

Prayer 23

Restoring God's Name in Our Culture

Religion that God our Father accepts as pure and faultless is this: to look after orphans and widows in their distress and to keep oneself from being polluted by the world.

James 1:27

Almighty God,

Not long ago our nation acknowledged You as the supreme authority of right and wrong, of good and evil, of righteousness and unrighteousness. We looked to You for guidance and relied upon Your Word for wisdom. And although we fell short, we still sought to anchor our country's moral underpinnings to You and Your Word.

As those biblical supports are now being pulled out of the soil of American mores, we plead for Your intervention.

Please forgive us for refusing to acknowledge Your hand in our nation's affairs. "Every good and perfect gift is from above." You have blessed us, and yet so often we turn our backs on You. Forgive our nation for exchanging the truth of God for a lie, and worshipping and serving created things rather than the Creator. Forgive us for relying on ourselves, for convincing ourselves that we are all we need.

Please show Yourself strong in our nation. Stir within us a love for You that repels our love for the world and everything in it — the cravings of sinful man, the lust of our eyes, and the boasting of what we have and do. You are the measure of all things; we are but a drop in the bucket.

By Your Holy Spirit convict us when we consciously or subconsciously remove Your influence from our culture. Give us the wisdom to know how to restore Your influence without becoming legalistic in the process.

Move within our media outlets so they will tell of Your

goodness and grace. Open our eyes and ears to identify Your truth that is revealed in our music, movies, and everyday events. At the same time extinguish the influences that run counter to Your holiness.

Through the election bring men and women to office who truly look to You for direction. May Your influence become greater and our influence lesser.

Yet may our nation not be content with merely living moral lives. Prevent us from equating morality with righteousness so that we deceive ourselves into thinking our works make us right before You. Only the perfect work of Jesus can make us right before the Father.

So heavenly Father, we welcome Your rightful place in our culture. Be enthroned in our midst.

Scripture references: Isaiah 40:15; John 3:30; Romans 1:25; James 1:17; 1 John 2:15-17

Read America's founding documents

Spend some time reading America's founding documents to understand the true meaning and intent of our democracy. Many people assume they know and understand all about the United States of America, but in fact are surprised to learn that many early Americans were committed Christians. The Declaration of Independence, The Bill of Rights, United States Constitution, Mayflower Compact, and even the Northwest Ordinance of 1787 all contain biblical language. To request copies of these documents, you can contact WallBuilders, an organization dedicated to the restoration of the moral and religious foundation in which America was built. Call 800-873-2845 or visit www.WallBuilders.com.

> *Good government generally begins in the family, and if the moral character of a people once degenerate, their political character must soon follow.*
>
> *—Elias Boudinot, 1795*

Prayer 24

Gay Rights

Therefore, as God's chosen people, holy and dearly loved, clothe yourselves with compassion, kindness, humility, gentleness and patience. Bear with each other and forgive whatever grievances you may have against one another. Forgive as the Lord forgave you. And over all these virtues put on love, which binds them all together in perfect unity.

Colossians 3:12-14

Almighty God,

Please stem the tide of homosexual rights in this nation. Although we can't dictate what takes place in our nation's bedrooms, we ask that You would prevent this lifestyle from being validated and forced upon us.

Living by our convictions in a culture where many despise them is quite a challenge. As followers of Your Son Jesus and believers in the authority of Your Word, we need Your wisdom. How do we restrain immorality without falling into legalism? To what extent do we stand up for our rights in light of the fact that Your Son Jesus emptied Himself of all rights when He came to earth? Most importantly, how can we show love in the midst of this?

You tell us that "the wisdom that comes from heaven is first of all pure; then peace-loving, considerate, submissive, full of mercy and good fruit, impartial and sincere. Peacemakers who sow in peace raise a harvest of righteousness." May Your church in America embody this kind of wisdom.

Forgive us for defining people by their sin and for often failing to show the indiscriminate love of Jesus Christ. Jesus, You never regarded anyone as untouchable, and neither should we. At the same time, please forgive us for allowing cultural mores and the fear of criticism to dictate the ardency of our stance toward homosexuality.

Please raise up candidates who believe in the authority of Your Word. When asked regarding their position on homosexuality, may You give them anointed answers that avoid easy accusations. At the same time, we know these candidates will not be able to avoid criticism altogether. Give them courage to speak the truth in love.

God, we look to You to redeem this situation. Please use the church as a balm of healing to so many homosexuals who have experienced tremendous pain and rejection in their past. Use our indiscriminate love and acceptance toward homosexuals to silence the issue of gay rights. And through us, may You bring healing and salvation.

Scripture references: Romans 1:26-27; Ephesians 3:15; Philippians 2:7; James 3:17-18

Support the Federal Marriage Amendment

Marriage is facing a hostile attack in our nation. Lawyers and activist judges are engaged in a massive effort to redefine marriage for our entire society. If you want to get involved in the fight to save marriage and the family, you can support the Federal Marriage Amendment. For information, contact the Alliance for Marriage Foundation, write P.O. Box 2490, Merrifield, Virginia, 22116, or visit www.allianceformarriage.org.

I believe there are more instances of the abridgement of the freedom of the people by gradual and silent encroachment of those in power than by violent and sudden usurpations.

—President James Madison, 1812

Prayer 25

Racial Reconciliation

Here there is no Greek or Jew, circumcised or uncircumcised, barbarian, Scythian, slave or free, but Christ is all, and is in all.

Colossians 3:11

Almighty God,

During Your ministry here on earth, You treated everyone with equity: Jew, Gentile, man, woman, demonized, diseased, disabled, and healthy. You modeled a love that mirrored the love of Your heavenly Father. And through the cross You obliterated all differences that divide. Obviously, discrimination has no place in Your kingdom.

Lord, we pray for our country. Our history of racism — both inside and outside the church — continues to divide us. Please give us wisdom to know how to deal with this volatile issue in a way that glorifies You.

Open our eyes to any vestiges of racism that still exist. Convict us by Your Holy Spirit to such a degree that we will feel compelled to dismantle from the structures of our society anything that unfairly discriminates according to the color of one's skin.

Jesus, You are in the business of bringing together the dividing walls of hostility. We look to You to bridge the racial gap with Your peace. In order for this to take place, we lay our preconceived ideas regarding racial prejudice at Your feet and ask for Your perspective.

May Your law of love govern those of us who have tasted privilege. Help us to proactively foster relationships with those who look different from us so we will understand them better. Move upon us with humility and generosity so we will willingly lay down any exclusive rights which should be shared.

At the same time we ask that You would inspire those of us who have tasted discrimination due to the color of our skin. Show us how to forgive so we aren't encumbered by our past, and give us a vision for the future that transcends any limitations we may place upon ourselves.

As we approach November 2, 2004, we ask that You would bless our nation with leaders who have fresh ideas — ideas that will bring us together. Ideas that empower and foster respect. So often, election results follow racial lines. This time, we ask that You would blur those lines and unify the American people — red, yellow, black, and white.

We need healing in our nation that only You can bring. Please model Your indiscriminate love through Your body, the church. May we be one as You are one with the Father and Holy Spirit. And through the love we share, may people encounter Jesus.

Scripture references: Matthew 8:1-4, 15:21-28; Luke 10:27; John 4:1-26, 17:21; Ephesians 2:14-16; Colossians 1:19-20, 3:11

Join a book club

Reading books is a great way to educate yourself on the issues. But with so many books (and so little time) how do you know which books you should read and which ones you shouldn't? One easy way to decide what to read is by joining a book club. You can rely on book clubs to help you find the most relevant and best-written books — all from the comfort of your own home. There are Christian book clubs, political book clubs, history book clubs, and others. Each club is managed by an editor who read the books to make recommendations you can trust.

I believe with all my heart that standing up for America means standing up for the God who has so blessed our land. We need God's help to guide our nation through stormy seas. But we can't expect Him to protect America in a crisis if we just leave Him over on the shelf in our day-to-day living.

—President Ronald Reagan, 1983

Prayer 26

Poverty

"Then the righteous will answer him, 'Lord, when did we see you hungry and feed you, or thirsty and give you something to drink? When did we see you a stranger and invite you in, or needing clothes and clothe you? When did we see you sick or in prison and go to visit you?' The King will reply, 'I tell you the truth, whatever you did for one of the least of these brothers of mine, you did for me.'"

Matthew 25:37-40

Almighty God,

Thank You for laying aside the riches of heaven to become one of us. From the very beginning of Your life here on earth You embodied Your name Immanuel — "God with us." The dusty manger, Your parents of simple means, the lowly shepherds proclaiming Your birth all point to the fact that Your love and presence extend to all people.

Your Word tells us that whenever we feed the hungry, give drink to the thirsty, invite the stranger into our homes, clothe the naked, visit the sick or the prisoner, we do it unto You. Every time we look into the face of the last and the least, we see You. Poverty isn't just an idea or income level, it's a face — Yours. Give us eyes to see that the way we respond to the underprivileged and disadvantaged is the way we respond to You.

You have blessed our nation, and we have become a relatively generous people. Help us to live in the realization that everything we have comes from You and belongs to You. "The earth is the Lord's, and everything in it, the world, and all who live in it."

Give our nation Your heart for the less fortunate and may we show Your compassion without judgmentalism or fault-finding.

As we approach the election, please guide the American voters to candidates with the ability to inspire generosity among the American people and the wisdom to empower and build dignity among the poor. Only with Your guidance can we walk through this labyrinth without straying into socialism or selfishness.

The wealth and pleasures we enjoy in our nation so easily seduce us. Deliver us from the idolatry of materialism and consumerism, and give us the power and will to live sacrificial lives just as You have with us.

Though You were rich, yet for our sakes You became poor, so that through Your poverty we might become rich. Thank You for extending the riches of Your love to me. Help me to follow Your example.

Scripture references: Psalm 24:1; Matthew 1:23, 25:40; 2 Corinthians 8:7-9

Host an Election Day "watch party"

One fun way to give your friends an extra incentive to vote is to announce a "watch party" at your home on November 2, 2004. Invite friends to come over, eat dinner or dessert, and watch the election returns as they come in across the nation. This is a good time to pray in agreement for God to move on behalf of the candidates who are victorious

> *For we must consider that we shall be as a City upon a hill. The eyes of all people are upon us. So that if we shall deal falsely with our God in this task we have undertaken, and so caused Him to withdraw His present help from us, we shall be made a story and a byword throughout the world.*
>
> *—John Winthrop, 1630*

Prayer 27

Education

Love the Lord your God with all your heart and with all your soul and with all your mind and with all your strength.

Mark 12:30

Almighty God,

The heavens declare Your glory, and the skies proclaim the work of Your hands. All around we behold Your fingerprints. Although Your glory is to conceal them, our glory is to search them out.

All wisdom and knowledge begin and end with You. And through them we find You, glorify You, and enjoy You. Obtaining a quality education may not be the chief end of man, but it *is* important for everyday living in our country. As we educate our children, please help us avoid falling short of its ultimate purpose: to know You and love You better.

Work within the hearts of our public school educators so they will allow students to practice their faith and share it with those around them. Like a magnet, attract godly men and women to our public schools who will model before our children a vibrant faith that is unafraid of any intellectual challenge. Give our administrators the courage to allow the free exchange of spiritual beliefs so we don't raise children who are educationally agnostic or atheist.

At the same time we ask that You would work through our Christian parents. Give them wisdom to know when to speak up and when to be silent. May their behavior persuade our public school officials to allow Christianity to flourish.

Through our Christian schools, build a solid biblical foundation for our students that will last them a lifetime. Jesus, may they encounter You in their studies to such a degree that they will avoid being inoculated against the effects of the gospel.

Thank You for our parents who invest in the lives of their children through home schooling. Encourage those parents who have made sacrifices on behalf of their children. When they're tired or overwhelmed, give them a vision of what the end product will look like. Use this opportunity as an incubation period so that their children will grow up to be adults who love Jesus and are comfortable engaging our culture.

Through the vote on November 2, 2004, we ask You to strengthen our educational system. Give our elected officials wisdom to know how to effectively steward the tax dollars earmarked for education. Raise our commitment to a standard that will provide a quality education to all people in our nation regardless of income, gender, or race. And in the process, renew their dedication to the development of character and the preservation of innocence. Help all of us to teach our children to choose the right path, so that when they are older, they will remain upon it.

Scripture references: Psalm 19:1; Proverbs 22:6, 25:2

Meetup!

The Internet now makes it possible for you to contact and meet with other like-minded people to discuss politics and to make a difference. Visit www.MeetUp.com and find a local group — or start your own group. MeetUp is a free service that enables people to organize local meetings. The groups are identified by issue and also by candidate. These meetings can be a great place to share your views and find other people who believe like you, and they can be a great place to meet new friends.

> *Our strength lies in spiritual concepts. It lies in public sensitiveness to evil. Our greatest danger is not from invasion by foreign armies. Our dangers are that we may commit suicide from within by complaisance with evil, or by public tolerance of scandalous behavior.*
>
> *—President Herbert Hoover, 1928*

Prayer 28

Judges and Our Judicial System

[Jehoshaphat] appointed judges in the land, in each of the fortified cities of Judah. He told them, "Consider carefully what you do, because you are not judging for man but for the Lord, who is with you whenever you give a verdict. Now let the fear of the Lord be upon you. Judge carefully, for with the Lord our God there is no injustice or partiality or bribery."

2 Chronicles 19:5-7

Almighty God,

What confidence we have in approaching You, whose throne is founded on righteousness and justice. When our feelings are moved by the changing winds of circumstances, You remain steadfast because You are the unchanging God.

You are the judge who not only metes out justice, but who is the definition of justice in a world of ever-changing definitions of right and wrong. And in the end, Your judgments will prove trustworthy and final.

As we approach the coming election we understand the implications of electing men and women to office: these men and women will directly affect and approve the people who will judge on Your behalf.

Please guide the American voters to candidates who believe in the rule of law. May they be men and women who look to You as the impartial arbiter of justice.

Lead our elected officials to judges endowed with the wisdom that comes from heaven — wisdom that is pure, peace-loving, considerate, submissive, full of mercy and good fruit, impartial, and sincere. Lead them to judges who love truth and choose life. Who prefer redemption over punishment. Who understand that no decision or person is greater than the laws You have established through Your Word.

When possible, may our judges render decisions and verdicts that are redemptive rather than punitive. Please immunize them against bribery, special interests, and undue criticism. And guide them with the conviction that they are accountable not only to the people, but also to You.

We especially pray for our next president, knowing that he will likely appoint judges to the bench of the Supreme Court. Guide us to the presidential candidate who fears You more than the latest poll or approval rating.

May the integrity and moral convictions of our presidential-appointed judges filter down throughout our justice system — from the Supreme Court to the appellate courts and to our individual municipalities.

May the words of the prophet Amos be fulfilled in our nation: "But let justice roll down like waters, and righteousness like an ever-flowing stream."

Scripture references: Numbers 23:19; Psalm 89:14; Proverbs 29:4; Isaiah 30:18; Daniel 4:37; Amos 5:24 NRSV; John 3:17; James 3:17

Concerned about our judiciary?

The Federalist Society is a group of citizens interested in the current state of the legal system. It is founded on the principles that the state exists to preserve freedom, that the separation of governmental powers is central to our Constitution, and that it is the duty of the judiciary to say what the law is, not what it should be. The Federalist Society provides opportunities for participation in the public policy process, and it has programs to encourage members to involve themselves in local and national judicial affairs. To join and interact with prominent officials in our legal system, call (202) 822-8138 or visit www.Fed-Soc.org.

Let not the foundation of our hope rest upon man's wisdom. It must be felt that there is no national security but in the Nation's humble, acknowledged dependence upon God and his overruling providence.
—President Franklin Pierce, 1835

Prayer 29

Foreign Policy

Blessed are the peacemakers, for they will be called sons of God.

Matthew 5:9

Almighty God,

You are the Prince of Peace, and through You we have peace with God. Thank You for bearing the wrath of our sins so we can know salvation.

We look forward to the day when we will experience true peace — when we will beat our swords into plowshares, when our earthly relationships will be reconciled, when we will enjoy an unhindered relationship with You. Yet we are content knowing we will have to wait until the end of the age before true peace is achieved.

In the meantime we pray for our country and her foreign policy. You tell us in Your Word to seek peace and pursue it, that wisdom is better than weapons of war. Through the upcoming election surround us with leaders who will seek a peace that transcends the lack of conflict and lean on Your wisdom to bring a relative freedom from hostility.

As we approach November 2, 2004, lead the voters to the presidential candidate who has the courage to stand up to other nations in the face of overwhelming criticism and the humility to back down on inconsequential issues. May our next president fully understand the responsibility of leading the world's most powerful country, and may he wisely and objectively act in the best interests of all concerned.

You encourage us to pray for the peace of Jerusalem. Please show our officials and mediators how to broker a peace that respects the dignity, history, and culture of the Jews and Palestinians. May our actions enhance — and not harm —

the witness of Your church in the Middle East.

Guide us as we rebuild Iraq and Afghanistan. Show us how to build stable, democratic countries that empower the people and suppress tyranny and religious oppression. Grant our officials in these countries favor in the eyes of the locals and the foresight to include the Iraqi and Afghan peoples in rebuilding their country.

Please give the American people a love and understanding for Muslims around the world. Monitor our words and actions so we will avoid unintentionally turning these people away from the gospel. Show us how we can love people well on the world's stage.

The number of foreign policy issues are endless: immigration, the status of illegal aliens, AIDS, trade inequities, world debt, poverty. We need godly leaders who have the mind of Christ so they will manifest Your wisdom. Please intensify within us a hunger for peace and the desire to act as bridge-builders — just as You have done for us.

Scripture references: Psalm 34:14, 122:6; Ecclesiastes 9:18; Isaiah 9:6; Micah 4:3-4; Matthew 24:6-8; John 14:27; Romans 5:1; Philippians 2:4

Call talk radio

Talk radio has become one of the most influential mediums in American politics. Millions of listeners tune in to hear debates and to make their views known. If you want to make your voice heard, give talk radio hosts a call. Make sure to call early in the show so you will be included in the program, write out your talking points to help you plan what you are going to say, and get to your point quickly when asked a question. You can contact local radio programs in your community or popular national hosts like Rush Limbaugh (800-282-2882), Sean Hannity (800-941-7326), Beverly LaHaye (800-527-9600), or Janet Parshall (800-343-9282).

Prayer changes lives and history. Praying for America's officials will empower them to provide inspired, courageous, moral leadership during the domestic and international crises facing all Americans.

—General John Wickham

Prayer 30

The Military

For he will command his angels concerning you to guard you in all your ways; they will lift you up in their hands, so that you will not strike your foot against a stone. You will tread upon the lion and the cobra; you will trample the great lion and the serpent.

Psalm 91:11-13

Almighty God,

You are a mighty warrior — You are strong in battle, skilled in combat, incisive in strategy, and the victory always belongs to You. With You as our defender, we need not be afraid. Thank You for being our refuge and strength, an ever-present help in trouble.

With American troops stationed around the globe, we ask that You would draw our service men and women under the shelter of Your wings. Be their refuge, their strength, their ever-present help in trouble. Be their defender, encourager, confidant, and friend. Please use the perilousness of their vocation to drive them to a saving knowledge of Jesus Christ.

With so many scattered throughout the world, we need a president who will fiercely defend our troops. Please lead the voters to the man who will be conscientiously concerned about the welfare and protection of those who defend our country. Give him the wisdom to utilize our troops so they aren't exposed to unnecessary harm. May our Commander-in-Chief inspire courage and greatness among those who follow him.

Please protect our troops from harm. Encamp Your angels around them and shield them from danger. Open their eyes to any potential terrorist threats that may endanger them or others. At the same time give them compassion for the people in whose countries they may be occupying. May they win the hearts of the locals — especially in Iraq and Afghanistan — and may they respect the dignity of both

Americans and non-Americans.

We also remember those men and women who serve stateside. Help them to see the importance of their jobs while defending America from within. Preserve the families that remain stateside while their spouses are serving overseas — guard these families from discouragement, dissension, and divorce.

We're grateful that our country allows Christian chaplains to serve alongside our men and women. Please blow Your fresh wind of the Holy Spirit over any spiritual dust that may have accumulated in their hearts. Lead them by Your Spirit so they will speak Your words into the lives of those in the military.

Last of all, we pray for those Christians who serve among our troops. Encourage them in their walk with You, and give them the strength to follow You in the face of temptation and ridicule. May their lives speak louder than their words, and through them, may others find salvation in Jesus Christ.

Scripture references: Exodus 15:3; Psalm 46:1, 61:4; Proverbs 21:31; Jeremiah 32:18

Vote early

Think you might be busy on Election Day? What if you get caught in traffic or have to work late on November 2, 2004? You don't have to wait until Election Day to vote. You can vote by absentee ballot in all 50 States. To cast your vote early, contact your local county or city election official. Also, this web link will take you to a site that will help you find the official sites of the Secretaries of State and/or Directors of Elections in your area: www.fvap.gov/links/statelinks.html.

The Almighty God has blessed our land in many ways. He has given our people stout hearts, and strong arms with which to strike mighty blows for freedom and truth. He has given to our country a faith which has become the hope of all peoples in an anguished world.
—President Franklin D. Roosevelt, 1939

Prayer 31

Terrorism

There are six things the Lord hates, seven that are detestable to him: haughty eyes, a lying tongue, hands that shed innocent blood, a heart that devises wicked schemes, feet that are quick to rush into evil, a false witness who pours out lies and a man who stirs up dissension among brothers.

Proverbs 6:16-19

Almighty God,

"When the foundations are being destroyed, what can the righteous do?"

On September 11, 2001, the foundation upon which our nation's security and safety was based was shaken. We now realize we no longer live in relative isolation and security.

As we approach November 2, 2004, please guard the United States from terrorist attack. Please place a hedge of protection around our president and political candidates during this dangerous season so that no foreign person or group will be able to influence the election.

Please guide Governor Tom Ridge and our Department of Homeland Security as they work to foil any terrorist plans. Secure our borders so that no one intent on destroying us will be able to enter. Give our customs officials extraordinary discernment so they will quickly identify any person or behavior that poses a legitimate threat to our nation's security. At the same time alert the Coast Guard to any suspicious activity that they may uncover malicious plans of destruction.

Direct our foreign intelligence operatives so they will be able to uncover any plots for harming our country. Only You can join the nations of our world together to oppose and uncover these evil men. Show the leaders of predominately Muslim countries that these terrorists pose a threat to them as well. Open the eyes of any sympathetic nations so they will see these people as they really are.

Thank You that we can rest in the fact that when the earth and all its people quake, You are the One who holds its pillars firm. Your name is a strong tower; the righteous run to it and are safe.

May we, the American people, avoid empowering any terrorist or terrorist organization through our fear. Instead, infuse us with courage as we learn to lean on You.

Please use the tragedy of September 11 to drive us to You. Through it may we rediscover the folly in assuming that we control our destiny. May the fire of September 11 be a purifying one for our nation — one that reminds us of our mortality and of Your divinity. One that reminds us that true security can only be found through salvation in Your son Jesus Christ.

Scripture references: Job 1:10; Psalm 11:3, 75:3; Proverbs 18:10;

College students can make a difference

Many college campuses are bastions of anti-American belief, but there are organizations for Christian students who want to get involved in campus politics. You can contact the Intercollegiate Studies Institute (ISI), a non-partisan organization whose purpose is to convey to successive generations of college students a better understanding of the values and institutions that sustain our liberties. Through its program of conferences and publications, it works with hundreds of thousands of students and faculty. For information, call 800-526-7022 or visit www.isi.org.

The Christian religion is the most important and one of the first things in which all children, under a free government aught to be instructed. No truth is more evident to my mind than that the Christian religion must be the basis of any government intended to secure the rights and privileges of a free people.

—Noah Webster, 1828

Prayers for the Hearts of the American People

Prayer 32

Sin and Crime

The people of the land practice extortion and commit robbery; they oppress the poor and needy and mistreat the alien, denying them justice. "I looked for a man among them who would build up the wall and stand before me in the gap on behalf of the land so I would not have to destroy it, but I found none.

Ezekiel 22:29-30

Almighty God,

It seems every day the problem of sin and crime looms larger in our country, while Your Word tells us, "Righteousness exalts a nation, but sin is a disgrace to any people."

Our problems with crime go much deeper than our outward actions. Our problem is our sinful nature: We crave what kills us. We desire what we do not have. We despise control. And we manipulate others in order to benefit ourselves. The minds and hearts of all people are cunning.

Lord God, we need men and women in office who are committed to seeing our nation exalted through righteousness. We need men and women who will stand in the gap on behalf of our land so that our selfish desires are prevented from bringing destruction and disgrace upon us.

Please lead us to the candidates endowed with a strong inward sense of right and wrong; candidates whose values align with Your Word. Candidates who desire to prevent and punish sin. Give them wisdom to know how to govern in a way that restrains wickedness and grant them eyes to see past the appearance and deal with our real need: You.

Through our elected officials may You foster a culture of compassion, generosity, honesty and integrity. Show them how to balance justice and mercy. "The Lord God has told us what is right and what He demands: 'See that justice is done, let mercy be your first concern, and humbly obey your God.'"

So often we barter wisdom for foolishness and the future for the present. Endow our officials with the foresight to sow long-term seeds that cultivate character and produce a harvest of righteousness.

Heavenly Father, You are the only one who can produce true change — change that begins on the inside and works its way out. May we become a people committed to You and may You in turn conform into the image of Your son, Jesus.

Scripture references: Psalm 64:6; Proverbs 14:34; Ezekiel 22:29-30; Micah 6:8 (CEV); John 17:25; Romans 1:22; Hebrews 12:11

Host a townhall meeting – in your own home

In early American history, candidates would travel from town to town to discuss their views in townhall meetings. That was the only way for them to get votes because in those days mail, telephones, and televisions didn't exist. Today, candidates still enjoy opportunities to meet voters face-to-face. If you want to get honest answers from a political candidate, invite them into your own home. Contact a local candidate and tell them you are inviting a group of friends to a neighborhood coffee. Most candidates like to meet voters face-to-face and will gladly come into your home. Invite lots of people and make it worth the candidate's time.

Whenever the pillars of Christianity shall be overthrown, our present Republican form of government, and all blessings which flow from them must fall with them.

—Jedediah Morse, 1799

Prayer 33

Unity in Our Nation

How good and pleasant it is when brothers live together in unity! It is like precious oil poured on the head, running down on the beard, running down on Aaron's beard, down upon the collar of his robes. It is as if the dew of Hermon were falling on Mount Zion. For there the Lord bestows his blessing, even life forevermore.

Psalm 133:1-3

Almighty God,

In the 228 years of our nation's history, we have encountered formidable threats to our existence. We have fought battles with swords and guns on fields of foreign soil — and we have also fought battles with words and ideas on the fields of American soil. From debates over states' rights to issues of slavery and human rights to civil rights, somehow our nation has remained intact. Thank You for holding the United States of America together.

On the heels of a presidential election laden with controversy and turmoil, we appeal to You: please keep our nation unified and strong. Please make Your will known to the American people through the election in a way that is clear and unmistakable.

However, should we face another contentious election as a result of November 2, 2004, we ask that You would bind the American people together. May our desire for unity and common purpose transcend our differences.

Your Word tells us that You hate those who sow discord. Silence anyone who willingly or unwillingly undermines our democracy by sowing seeds of rebellion or anarchy.

Protect the election process so that our electors, delegates, election workers, judges, and other public officials will avoid even a hint of misconduct. Place a guard over the mouths of the losing candidates and supporters of losing causes so that their words and actions avoid dividing the victors from the American people. May we all be committed to one another and to our system of government regardless of who wins the vote.

Please use our president and other elected officials to bring our people together as one while allowing for the diversity that has made our nation great. Together may they build a foundation that stabilizes our country like never before.

"Hatred stirs up dissension, but love covers over all wrongs." May Your Son Jesus be lifted up as the model of sacrificial love that brings unity and peace.

Scripture references: Proverbs 6:16, 10:12, Romans 16:17; 1 Corinthians 1:10; 1 Thessalonians 5:23

Contact a lobbyist

Although the term "lobbyist" has no legal definition, it usually refers to someone who is paid to represent special interest groups. There are pro-life lobbyists, anti-tax lobbyists, pro-family lobbyists, and others. One prominent Christian lobbyist organization is the National Association of Evangelicals (NAE). Lobbyists know the intricacies of government and meet with legislators on a regular basis. They push for certain bills to be passed or form alliances with other groups to defeat a bill. Legislators rely on lobbyists to help them make decisions on issues, because they know lobbyists represent large groups of voters. If you are concerned about an issue that affects Christians, contact the NAE at (202) 789-1011 or visit www.nae.net and make your voice heard.

In no other way can this republic become a world power in the noblest sense of the word than by putting into Her life and the lives of Her citizens the spirit and principles of the Great Founder of Christianity.

—David J. Brewer,
Justice of the U.S. Supreme Court, 1901

Prayer 34

God's Blessing on America

David says the same thing when he speaks of the blessedness of the man to whom God credits righteousness apart from works: "Blessed are they whose transgressions are forgiven, whose sins are covered. Blessed is the man whose sin the Lord will never count against him."

Romans 4:6-8

Almighty God,

You have blessed Your people far beyond comprehension. When we were spiritually poor, You made us rich. When we were dead in our sins, You made us alive with You. When we were in conflict with our heavenly Father, You became our reconciliation. When we were outcasts, you became our means of adoption into Your family. When we needed salvation, You saved us. In love, You have held nothing back from us — not even Your life.

Thank You for rescuing us from the dominion of darkness and bringing us into Your kingdom. You have freed us from bondage to sin and led us into the Promised Land of forgiveness, eternal life, and true freedom. Thank you for blessing us with every spiritual blessing in Christ: When we have You we have everything — we are truly blessed!

With this in mind, we make this request: God bless America! Bless us with the privilege of knowing and loving You. Bless us with the eternal favor that comes from a relationship with You. Bless us so that we can bless the nations of the earth with the good news of Jesus Christ.

May our nation's greatest source of boasting be this: that we understand and know You. Place a longing within Your church to avoid a return to revivals of the past. What we need is a new movement of Your Spirit. A movement that surpasses previous moves. A movement that embodies Your love and holiness. A movement that affects change in the hearts of the American people.

May our nation experience the blessed life that comes to those who are poor in spirit, who mourn their sin, who are meek, who hunger and thirst for righteousness, who show mercy, who are pure in heart, peacemakers, and persecuted for righteousness' sake. Blessed is the nation whose God is the Lord!

So we ask that You would use the November 4 election to bring us to that place of blessing. To that place where we realize our need for You. To that place where we seek first Your kingdom and Your righteousness, knowing that when we do so, everything else that we need will be added as well.

Scripture references: Psalm 33:12; Isaiah 43:19; Jeremiah 9:24; Matthew 5:3-12, 6:33; John 8:36; Romans 5:10, 8:17; 2 Corinthians 8:9; Ephesians 1:3, 5; Colossians 1:13-14, 2:13

How do you know what to believe?

Do you trust the news media? The press has no enforceable code of ethics for professional conduct. A lawyer who lies can be jailed for contempt of court. A surgeon who messes up an operation can lose his license. A corporation that falsifies reports can face serious troubles with the SEC. However, a journalist doesn't have to surrender his press card for faulty reporting. Accuracy In Media is a grassroots citizens watchdog of the news media that critiques botched and bungled news stories and sets the record straight on important issues that have received slanted coverage. We encourage members of the media to report the news fairly and objectively—without resorting to bias or partisanship.

Intoxicated with unbroken success, we have become too self-sufficient to feel the necessity of redeeming and preserving grace, too proud to pray to the God that made us! It behooves us then to humble ourselves before the offended Power, to confess our national sins and to pray for clemency and forgiveness.
—President Abraham Lincoln, 1864

Prayer 35

Godly Motives

Since, then, you have been raised with Christ, set your hearts on things above, where Christ is seated at the right hand of God. Set your minds on things above, not on earthly things. For you died, and your life is now hidden with Christ in God.

Colossians 3:1-3

The goal of this command is love, which comes from a pure heart and a good conscience and a sincere faith.

1 Timothy 1:5

Almighty God,

Time and space cannot contain Your greatness. You have searched us and known us. You know when we sit and when we rise; You perceive our thoughts from afar. You discern our going out and our lying down; You are familiar with all our ways. Before a word is on our tongues You know it completely.

You also know that our thoughts are futile and our hearts are deceitful above all things. Even our best attempts at serving You are dappled with selfishness and pride.

Jesus, thank You for dwelling in Your church. It's amazing that You would choose not only to save us, but to work through us. Our only fitting response is to worship You with our lives.

Examine our hearts and motives. Move Your people so they will seek Your heart before casting their votes. Because we belong to You we desire to hold nothing back from You — so tear down any walls of assumptions or preconceived ideas we might have that only serve as edifices unto ourselves. Convict us when we allow our flesh to drown out Your Spirit's voice in the decisions we make.

Provoke Your people to vote from an eternal perspective. Bring back to our remembrance that this earth is not our home; we are merely aliens and strangers. Stir within us that longing for a better country embedded in the heart of every believer.

May the votes we cast on November 2 glorify You more than serve us. May they spring from a pure heart, a good conscience, and a sincere faith. Most of all, may love be our guide as we, Your body, go to the polls.

Scripture references: Psalm 94:11, 139:1-4; Isaiah 64:6; Jeremiah 17:9; Colossians 1:15; Hebrews 11:13,16

Pastors can get involved too

According to Crown Financial Ministries, a church should not endorse or support any political candidate or party. A church should not distribute campaign literature, raise money for candidates, or do anything to persuade church-goers to vote a particular way. But this does not mean pastors should opt out of the American democratic system entirely. Churches, ministries, and religious organizations can sponsor debates or forums to educate voters where all candidates are treated equally. They also can conduct voter registration or get-out-and-vote campaigns as long as they do not use these efforts to promote, denounce, or endorse particular issues, candidates, or political parties.

History is cluttered with the wreckage of nations that became indifferent to God, and died.

—Whittaker Chambers, 1952

Prayer 36

Godly Dependence

Open the gates that the righteous nation may enter, the nation that keeps faith. You will keep in perfect peace him whose mind is steadfast, because he trusts in you. Trust in the Lord forever, for the Lord, the Lord, is the Rock eternal.

Isaiah 26:2-4

Almighty God,

Amidst the flurry of election activity — the claims of candidates, the implications of referendums, the commentaries of political pundits — the temptation is to look to this present life for meaning. When our candidates or referendums lose, we easily get discouraged and fall into the assumption that America is disintegrating. And when they win, we feel encouraged and believe that America is getting stronger. It's so easy to place our hope in this present life.

Forgive us, Lord God, when we worship and serve creation rather than the Creator. Forgive us when we look to our system of government as god and depend on it rather than You. You tell us in Your Word: "Cursed is the one who trusts in man, who depends on flesh for his strength and whose heart turns away from the Lord." Regardless of the outcome of the November 2 election, may we turn away from dependence on the flesh and may we look to You for provision, protection, and guidance.

Your hand in the formation and guidance of this country is unmistakable. Nevertheless, may our love for You and our allegiance to You always override our love and allegiance to the United States of America. We choose to obey You rather than any human invention.

We refuse to place our trust in people who cannot save us. Rather, we look to You to place righteous men and women in positions of authority in this nation.

We look to You as our defender. "Some trust in chariots and

some in horses, but we trust in the name of the Lord our God." You are the One who gives us victory and puts our adversaries to shame.

We look to You as our provider. Living in the wealthiest country in human history, the temptation is to place our hope in our wealth. But, God, we place our hope in You — the One who richly provides us with everything for our enjoyment.

We look to You as our judge. Through Your Son, You are the only One who can judge with impartiality, justice, and finality.

Hear our prayer and draw our nation into greater dependence on You. May we embody the truth of Jeremiah 17:7-8:

> *But blessed is the man who trusts in the Lord, whose confidence is in him. He will be like a tree planted by the water that sends out its roots by the stream. It does not fear when heat comes; its leaves are always green. It has no worries in a year of drought and never fails to bear fruit.*

Scripture references: Psalm 20:7, 31:15, 44:6-7; Jeremiah 17:5, 31:33; John 5:22, 30; Acts 5:29; Romans 1:25; 1 Timothy 6:17; 1 Peter 1:17

Write a book

If you're a writer, you could write a book about a local or national issue. Phyllis Schlafly self-published a book in 1968 called *A Choice, Not an Echo*, which sold millions of copies. As a result, Schlafly was named one of the 100 most important women of the 20th century by the *Ladies' Home Journal.* New publishing technologies make it easy for you to get published and promote your own book to bookstores and on the Internet. Contact Xulon Press at 1-866-381-2665 or visit www.XulonPress.com.

> *The foundations of our society and our government rest so much on the teachings of the Bible that it would be difficult to support them if faith in these teachings would cease to be practically universal in our country.*
> *—President Calvin Coolidge, 1921*

Prayer 37

Furthering of the Gospel

I urge, then, first of all, that requests, prayers, intercession and thanksgiving be made for everyone—for kings and all those in authority, that we may live peaceful and quiet lives in all godliness and holiness. This is good, and pleases God our Savior, who wants all men to be saved and to come to a knowledge of the truth.

1 Timothy 2:1-4

Almighty God,

Every election brings with it the prospect of change to our nation — not only a change in candidates and issues, but a change that potentially affects the welfare and morality of our nation. Yet, God, the welfare and morality of our nation are not enough. We need hearts that are changed, hearts that turn to You.

Please work through the November 2 election to further Your kingdom. Cultivate the spiritual landscape in our country so that our hearts become fertile soil for the gospel. Write Your law in our minds and on our hearts so that You will be our God and we will be Your people.

Speak to the American people through our candidates and referendum issues. Reveal the presence of Your truth — or the lack of it — to point to the foundation of truth, which is Your Word, and Your Son Jesus, who embodies Your Word and Your truth. Open our eyes to the bankruptcy of living lives apart from You and the consequences that unrighteousness brings.

Speak to the American people through Your church. May we not be content with merely voting in the election, but mobilize us and send us into the political arenas so we will be salt and light in our communities. Our prayer is not that You would take us out of the world but that You would protect us from the evil one in the midst of it.

Give us the words to clearly proclaim the good news of salvation in Jesus. Grant us wisdom so we will know how to act toward people who don't yet know You — so we will make the most of every opportunity. Season our conversations with grace, so that we will know how to answer everyone.

Do what it takes to reach our country. Whether a tragedy, surprise, or success, use any circumstances necessary to bring our nation to the place where people realize their need for You.

Most of all, please pour out the conviction of Your Holy Spirit on our nation so we will be aware of the immensity of our sin and our need for Jesus.

Scripture references: Jeremiah 31:33; Matthew 5:13-16, 9:38; John 17:15; Colossians 4:4-6

Contact the White House

If you support or oppose the president of the United States on an issue, or if you want to let your voice be heard on an issue you feel the president should address, you can contact the White House directly.

Mail a letter to the White House:

The White House
1600 Pennsylvania Ave, NW
Washington, DC 20500

Call or fax the White House:

Comments: 202-456-1111
Switchboard: 202-456-1414
Fax: 202-456-2461
E-mail the White House:
president@whitehouse.gov

Liberty cannot be established without morality, nor morality without faith.
—Alexis de Tocqueville, 1851

Prayer 38

His Kingdom Come and His Will Be Done

This, then, is how you should pray: "Our Father in heaven, hallowed be your name, your kingdom come, your will be done on earth as it is in heaven..."

Matthew 6:9-10

Almighty God,

You have been so good to me. Thank You for rescuing me from the dominion of darkness and bringing me into Your kingdom. Only in You do I find redemption and the forgiveness of sins.

When I think about Your sacrificial love for me I'm inspired not only to live for You, but to lay down my life for You as well. More important than the fulfillment of my wants and needs, more important than seeing my preferred candidates elected or my ballot initiatives succeed, is seeing Your kingdom come and Your will done. Please show me how I can join You in furthering Your kingdom.

Move in the hearts of Your people so we will lay down our comforts, biases, preferences, and wants for the sake of the kingdom. We seek first Your kingdom and Your righteousness, knowing that when we do so, everything else will be given to us as well.

Work through Your church so that the good news of the kingdom will be proclaimed with boldness. May our words and actions reflect Your kingdom work in our lives. We offer ourselves as agents of Your healing and reconciliation. Freely we have received so freely we give.

Through Your work in us, may we see the downfall of Satan's kingdom. Help us to believe that You are the answer to poverty, war, violence, oppression, demonization, sickness, and disease. Through us may America and the world know the life-changing, all-encompassing love of Jesus

Christ. Empower us to continue Your kingdom work.

Use the election to cultivate the hearts of the American people so they will respond with openness and joy to the good news of salvation. Use our ballot initiatives and candidates to spur the planting of churches and the sending out of missionaries. May we witness in our generation the unhindered rule and reign of God. May we witness eternity breaking into our human existence.

At the same time we ask that You would guard Your church from falling into triumphalism. The battle isn't ours, it's Yours. The victory isn't ours, it's Yours. But we commit ourselves to working until the day when we will join with the voices in heaven to proclaim:

> *"The kingdom of the world has become the kingdom of our Lord and of his Christ, and he will reign for ever and ever."*

Scripture references: Matthew 6:33, 9:35, 10:8, 24:14; Luke 10:17-19; John 18:36; Colossians 1:13-14; Revelation 11:15

How to involve your children

Getting your whole family involved in a political campaign is a great way to educate your kids on the American political process — and a lot of fun. Campaigns are always looking for help stuffing envelopes, licking stamps, or even marching in parades and passing out balloons to other children. There's no better school than the school of experience, so choose a good cause or candidate and get involved. For additional resources, you can contact Generation Joshua, founded by Michael P. Farris. Generation Joshua helps kids get involved in the political process. Young people can make a difference in the political arena, even if they aren't old enough to vote! For information visit www.GenerationJoshua.com.

The highest glory of the American Revolution was this; it connected, in one indissoluble bond the principles of civil government with the principles of Christianity.

—John Quincy Adams, 1822

Prayer 39

God's Glory in the Election

"Now my heart is troubled, and what shall I say? 'Father, save me from this hour'? No, it was for this very reason I came to this hour. Father, glorify your name!" Then a voice came from heaven, "I have glorified it, and will glorify it again."

John 12:27-28

Almighty God,

In this life, we will never be able to comprehend how loving, how merciful, how holy, how beautiful, how great You are. All around us we see shadows of You. Shadows that point to the immensity of Your holiness and love. "The heavens declare the glory of God; the skies proclaim the work of his hands."

Since creation Your invisible qualities — Your eternal power and divine nature — have been clearly seen. Believer or unbeliever, none of us is without excuse, and all of us will someday bow down at the feet of Jesus. Regardless of our acknowledgment of You in this life, this we know: You *will* glorify Your name.

Despite the inevitable, I *choose* to glorify Your name. More important than seeing my candidate or my cause win is seeing Your Son Jesus lifted up. Regardless of the outcome of the November 2 election, I choose to give You praise. Be glorified in my actions, my reactions, my words, my thoughts, my intentions. Let Your light shine through me before all people, so that they may see my good deeds and praise my Father in heaven.

Be glorified through our candidates, our ballot initiatives, and the media. Open our eyes to see Your hand in the election, and open the eyes of America to see the beauty of Jesus.

I look forward to the day when a multitude from every nation, tribe, people, and language will stand before the throne and the Lamb and cry, "Salvation belongs to our

God, who sits on the throne, and to the Lamb."

Our salvation comes from You — not from a political cause nor from any person. Even the random events and trivial occurrences find their beginning in You. So, Lord God, I glorify You because You are the One who holds the universe together, who sets kings on their thrones and grants salvation to even the most undeserving. You are the One who saves me through the blood of Jesus. I choose to worship You.

Scripture references: 1 Kings 10:9; Psalm 19:1, 24:7, 46:8-10, 86:9-10; Proverbs 16:4; Matthew 5:16; John 12:32; Romans 1:20; Philippians 2:9-11; 1 Corinthians 10:31; Revelation 7:9-10

Use the World Wide Web

All the political information you could ever want (and more!) is on the Internet for you to research. Articles, position papers, petitions, polls, and surveys — even ideas for contributing time and money — are available online. You can also attend online candidate forums and chat events, or e-mail friends and family to encourage them to get involved. It's not hard to find sites about politics, but be careful to find out the nature of the site you're visiting and who owns it. A good place to start is www.TownHall.com or www.WorldNetDaily.com.

I believe in the Holy Scriptures, and whoso lives by them will be benefited thereby. Men may differ as to the interpretation, which is human, but the Scriptures are man's best guide.

—Ulysses S. Grant, 1865

Prayer 40

God's Truth Will Prevail

The elder, to the chosen lady and her children, whom I love in the truth—and not I only, but also all who know the truth—because of the truth, which lives in us and will be with us forever.

2 John 1-2

Almighty God,

Thank You that regardless of the outcome of the November 2 election, we need not worry or fret about who is in control. Long before the heavens and earth were created You were here, and long after it has passed away You will still be here.

"The grass withers, the flower fades, but the word of our God stands forever." In the face of changing morals and designer beliefs we need not fear because the Word of our God stands forever. In the face of dishonest and amoral politicians who continue to be reelected, we need not fear because the Word of our God stands forever. In the face of disintegrating families and churches that are silent regarding issues of sin, we need not fear because the Word of our God stands forever.

Jesus, You are the Word of God incarnate, the way, the truth, and the life, the mediator of truth who guides us into all truth. You are the One who will judge the world in righteousness and the peoples in Your truth. You are the same, yesterday, today, and forever. Jesus, we have nothing to fear because the battle with falsehood is already over. We thank You that You not only defeated Satan, the father of lies, but You made a public spectacle of him, triumphing over him by the cross

We have nothing to fear, Jesus, because You are truth, You defeated falsehood, and You will live forever.

"Now we see but a poor reflection as in a mirror; then we

shall see face to face. Now I know in part; then I shall know fully, even as I am fully known." We look forward to the day when we will see from Your perspective, when we will know the truth because we know You fully. But in the meantime, we will be content to trust that You are in control and Your truth will ultimately win.

Scripture references: Psalm 96:13; Isaiah 40:8 (NASB95); Jeremiah 10:10; John 1:14, 17, 8:44, 14:6, 16:13; 1 Corinthians 13:12; Colossians 2:15; Hebrews 13:8

How to Contact Congress

To find your senators' and representatives' phone numbers, call the U.S. Capitol switchboard at 202-224-3121 and ask for your senators and/or representative. Remember that telephone calls are usually taken by a staff member, not the member of Congress. Ask to speak with the aide who handles the issue about which you wish to comment. After identifying yourself, tell the aide you would like to leave a brief message. You will also want to state reasons for your support or opposition to the bill. Ask for your senators' or representatives' position on the bill. You may also request a written response to your telephone call. Don't forget to be polite, even if you strongly disagree with a position or vote.

If the Church languishes, the State cannot be in health; and if the State rebels against its Lord and King, the Church cannot long enjoy its favor. I charge you, citizens of the United States, afloat on your wide sea of politics. There is another king, one Jesus. The safety of the State can be secured only in the way of humble loyalty to His person and of obedience to His law.

—Archibald Alexander Hodge, 1876

Key Races of the 2004 Election

Less than a year from now, after all the stump speeches, conventions, debates, and news stories, we will either have a new president, or voters will have returned George W. Bush to the White House. But there are also many other important decisions to be made on November 2, 2004, besides the Presidency.

Many political observers say that more than perhaps any other election in modern history, the 2004 race could change the course of the United States of America. That is because the government is currently evenly divided between Republicans and Democrats. If either party takes a majority of the races on November 2, we would soon see a major shift in the kinds of laws that get passed and enforced.

The Issues

What is at stake in 2004? From cultural issues to war and the economy, our political leaders will make many important and historical decisions after they are elected.

There are a myriad of social and cultural issues being debated in legislatures and courts across the country including same-sex marriage, the right to life, the acknowledgement of God's name in public places, pornography in the media, stem cell research, and the freedom to worship freely. Will the pledge of allegiance be altered to take away the phrase "under God?" Will the Ten Commandments be posted in public places, or ordered to be torn down? Will homosexual couples be allowed to adopt children? These are the questions our leaders will be answering for us.

Of course, there is the salient issue of terrorism. Our freedoms and liberties have never been at so much at risk, both here and abroad. The leaders we elect will decide how to fight the war on terror to prevent future attacks on our country. Who do you trust to right the war on terror? Which party will best protect America?

The economy and domestic issues are also high on the agenda. Some of our political leaders want to solve domestic issues with higher taxes and more government, while others prefer lower taxes and less government. Did you know most working Americans spend nearly 5 of 12 months out the year just making enough money to pay their taxes? So if you think taxes aren't a major voting issue, check your pay stubs! Who you vote for on November 2, 2004 will probably have a direct impact on your paycheck.

Finally, other domestic issues such as health care, welfare, crime, and the environment are high on the list of every candidate running for office.

Who will decide these issues?

It's not just the President and Vice-President who play an integral role in the issues. There are important races in the United States House of Representatives and Senate. Also, many states will elect a new governor. Although races for governor aren't considered national races, governors play a key role in how your tax dollars are spent where you live.

The United States Senate

The current balance in the Senate is 51 Republicans, 48 Democrats and one Independent who generally votes with Democrats. This means the Senate is evenly divided. In 2004, 15 Republican and 19 Democratic seats will be contested. Of these, 8 of the seats are being vacated by retiring Senators. With five Southern Democrats retiring, the South seems poised to help Republicans add to their two-vote majority in the U.S. Senate. Of course, there is no way to know how voters will cast their votes on November 2, 2004.

The following races will be hotly contested, either because there is no incumbent running for re-election (these are called open seats) or because the current incumbent is running for in a state divided evenly between Republicans and Democrats. If you reside in one of these states, it's time to pray and get involved:

ALASKA

Republican Senator Frank Murkowski was elected governor in 2002 and then named his daughter, Lisa Murkowski, as successor after the gubernatorial oath. Democrats have responded by coming up with a strong challenger, former Governor Tony Knowles. No Democrat has won a Senate seat here since 1974.

COLORADO

Republican Senator, Ben Nighthorse Campbell, is retiring due to health problems. Democratic state Attorney General Salazar will run, probably against former congressman Bob Schaffer – a Republican. This could be the closest and most watched race for Senate in 2004 as Colorado is evenly divided between Democrats and Republicans.

FLORIDA

Long-time Democratic Senator, Bob Graham, is retiring.

This seat was Graham's for as long as he wanted it, but after briefly seeking sought the 2004 Democratic presidential nomination, he decided to call it quits. President Bush's Secretary of the Interior, Mel Martinez is running for the Republican nomination, along with former Congressman Bill McCollum, former New Hampshire Senator Bob Smith, and others. This is a critical race because the race for President in 2000 was decided in Florida.

GEORGIA

Zell Miller, a conservative Democrat is retiring. Republicans could gain this seat back as Georgians have voted strongly in favor of Republican during the last few elections – and with Zell Miller weighing in on the side of President George W. Bush, it could be an uphill battle for Democrats in Georgia. Reps. Johnny Isakson and Mac Collins are vying for the Republican nomination, along with Godfather Pizza CEO Herman Cain, while the Democrats seemed to have given up on the seat as no prominent Democratic candidates are even running.

ILLINOIS

Peter Fitzgerald, a Republican, is leaving office after only one term. He unseated the Carol Moseley Braun six years ago, but by the barest of margins. The Democrats nominated Barack Obama, who if he wins would become only the third African American sent to the Senate since Reconstruction. The Republican candidate is Jack Ryan, a millionaire investment banker-turned-inner-city schoolteacher.

LOUISIANA

A unique situation presents itself in Louisiana, where several Democratic candidates will run against a single Republican, and if no candidate achieves 50 percent, they will head to a run-off to replace retiring Democratic Sen.

John Breaux. Two congressmen, Republican David Vitter and Democrat Chris John, jumped into the race soon after Breaux's announcement. Others are either already running or are contemplating getting in. Republicans have never won a Louisiana Senate seat.

NORTH CAROLINA

John Edwards gave up a re-election run to concentrate on his presidential bid; now, his best hope may be a spot on the John Kerry ticket. Erskine Bowles, President Clinton's one-time chief of staff, lost a Senate race against Elizabeth Dole in 2002 and is trying again. The Republican nominee will probably be Congressman Richard Burr – a close ally of the Bush administration. North Carolina tends to elect Republicans to the Senate in Presidential years

OKLAHOMA

Conservative Senator, Don Nickles, is retiring. Nickles is well-known for his strong pro-life positions. Oklahoma tends to vote Democratic in local elections, but usually opts for Republican candidates in state wide elections. Three serious candidates are vying for the Republican nomination in Oklahoma, Oklahoma City Mayor Kirk Humphreys, Rep. Tom Coburn and State Corporation Commissioner Bob Anthony. The likely Democratic nominee will be Rep. Brad Carson.

SOUTH CAROLINA

Ernest Hollings, a Democrat, is calling it quits after nearly 40 years in the Senate (he was elected during the Kennedy administration). Without the advantage of Hollings' incumbency, Democratic attempts to hold onto this seat could be an uphill climb. South Carolina is now the most Republican of all Southern states. The dynamics of the race on the Republican side changed when former Governor

David Beasley entered, joining Congressman Jim DeMint and former Attorney General Charlie. State Education Secretary Inez Tenenbaum is the likely nominee on the Democratic side.

SOUTH DAKOTA

The Senate minority leader, Tom Daschle, will seek a fourth term. Standing in his way is former congressman John Thune, whose bid for the Senate two years ago fell short by just 524 votes! This race will be watched closely and we can be sure many millions of dollars will be poured into this critical race.

These remaining Senators will all face re-election on November 2, 2004:

- Bayh, Even IN
- Bennett, Robert UT
- Bond, Christopher MO
- Boxer, Barbara CA
- Brownback, Sam KS
- Bunning, Jim KY
- Crapo, Mike, ID
- Dodd, Christopher CT
- Dorgan, Byron ND
- Feingold, Russell WI
- Grassley, Chuck IA
- Inouye, Daniel HI
- Judd, Craig NH
- Leahy, Patrick VT
- Lincoln, Blanche AR
- McCain, John AZ
- Mikulski, Barbara MD
- Murray, Patty WA
- Reid, Harry NV
- Schumer, Charles NY
- Shelby, Richard AL

- Spector, Arlen PA
- Voinovich, George OH
- Wyden, Ron OR

House of Representatives

There are 435 seats in the House of Representatives. Since a seat in the House is always held for only 2 years, all 435 seats will be up for election in 2004. The current balance in the House is 229 Republicans, 205 Democrats, and one Independent who aligns with Democrats. According to most political observers there will be little change in the overall make-up of the House of Representatives, mostly due to the fact that incumbent candidates almost always win (in 2002 more than 90% of all incumbent candidates were re-elected!). But there will be some "hotly"contested open seats (seats that will no longer be held by incumbents) due to the retirement or, in a few cases, the death of the current Congressman.

Governors

Currently, Republican governors hold 27 seats and Democrats hold 23 seats. Among the governors up for election in 2004, five are Republicans and six are Democrats. States electing governors in 2004 are Delaware, Indiana, Missouri, Montana, North Carolina, North Dakota, New Hampshire, Utah, Vermont, Washington, and West Virginia. Each State has its own schedule, but many of them plan their statewide and municipal elections on the same day as federal elections. Here is a summary of the most important gubernatorial races:

Indiana

Indiana's gubernatorial race has taken interesting turns due to the death of Governor Frank O'Bannon. Lt. Governor Joe Kernan was appointed Governor after O'Bannon's death, and will now face former Office of Management and

Budge (OMB) director Mitch Daniels, who left office to run in this race and has the backing of President Bush.

Missouri

Incumbent Gov. Bob Holden is running for reelection, but will probably face state Auditor Claire McCaskill in a tough primary race, given his low approval rating. The likely GOP nominee is Missouri's 32-year-old Secretary of State – Matt Blunt, the son of Rep. Roy Blunt. Missouri always has close races because it is evenly decided between Republicans and Democrats.

North Carolina

North Carolina tends to elect Republicans to the Senate in Presidential years. Gov. Mike Easley is running for reelection and many Republicans have piled into the race including former Charlotte Mayor Richard Vinroot, former state GOP Chairman Bill Cobey, state Senate Minority Leader Patrick Ballantine, Southern Pines businessman George Little, and Davie County commissioner Dan Barrett.

Washington

Gov. Gary Locke, considered a rising star in the Democratic party, surprised everyone by announcing that he would not run for reelection. Democrats who quickly decided to launch gubernatorial bids include state Attorney General Christine Gregoire, King County Executive Ron Sims, and former state Supreme Court Justice Phil Talmadge. State Sen. Dino Rossi is the frontrunner and will probably be the Republican nominee.

West Virginia

Gov. Bob Wise has decided not to seek reelection to heal the wounds caused by an extramarital affair. Following his announcement, former state Sen. Lloyd Jackson began seeking the Democratic nomination, joining Secretary of State Joe Manchin and others. At least 9 Republicans are also vying for their party's nomination.

Montana

Faced with a low approval rating, Gov. Judy Martz recently announced that she will not run for reelection. Republican candidates include former state Sen. Ken Miller, state Sen. Tom Keating, Secretary of State Bob Brown, and businessman Pat Davison. Rancher Brian Schweitzer is the only Democrat running so far, but Gallatin County Commissioner John Vincent is considering the race.

Utah

With Gov. Mike Leavitt's appointment to the Environmental Protection Agency (EPA), the race for his seat opened up and many candidates quickly emerged. Utah's new governor, Olene Walker, hasn't announced her intentions, but seven other Republicans have jumped in. The only announced Democrat so far is Scott Matheson, Jr., son of the former governor.

A Guide to the Electoral College

According to our Constitution, the president is not chosen by a nationwide popular vote. It's the electoral vote that determines the winner. Electoral votes are awarded on the basis of the popular vote in each state. The candidate who gets the most votes in your state will get *all* the electoral votes of your state. Conversely the candidate who gets the least votes won't get any electoral votes from your state. The candidate who reaches 270 electoral votes wins the presidency.

It's a "winner take all" system referred to as the Electoral College. Under the Electoral College system, the presidential election is decided by the combined results of 51 state elections (50 states and the District of Columbia). But your vote helps decide which candidate receives your state's electoral votes.

The founding fathers devised the Electoral College as part of their plan to share power between the states and the national government. Under the federal system adopted in the Constitution, the nationwide popular vote has no legal significance. As a result, it is possible that the electoral votes awarded on the basis of state elections could produce a different result from the nationwide popular vote (this happened in the 2000 elections when President George W. Bush lost the nation's popular vote but won a majority of the electoral votes).

The number of electoral votes allotted to each state corresponds to the number of representatives and senators that each state sends to Congress. In the Electoral College, each state gets one electoral vote for each of its representatives in the House, and one electoral vote for each of its two senators. Thus, every state has at least three electoral votes, because the Constitution grants each state two senators and at least one representative. In addition to the 535 electoral votes divided among the states, the District of Columbia has three electoral votes. Here is a state by state breakdown of how many electoral votes each state will cast in the 2004 election:

ALABAMA	9	MONTANA	3
ALASKA	3	NEBRASKA	5
ARIZONA	10	NEVADA	5
ARKANSAS	6	NEW HAMPSHIRE	4
CALIFORNIA	55	NEW JERSEY	15
COLORADO	9	NEW MEXICO	5
CONNECTICUT	7	NEW YORK	31
DELAWARE	3	NORTH CAROLINA	15
DC	3	NORTH DAKOTA	3
FLORIDA	27	OHIO	20
GEORGIA	15	OKLAHOMA	7
HAWAII	4	OREGON	7
IDAHO	4	PENNSYLVANIA	21
ILLINOIS	21	RHODE ISLAND	4
INDIANA	11	SOUTH CAROLINA	8
IOWA	7	SOUTH DAKOTA	3

KANSAS	6	TENNESSEE	11
KENTUCKY	8	TEXAS	34
LOUISIANA	9	UTAH	5
MAINE	4	VERMONT	3
MARYLAND	10	VIRGINIA	13
MASSACHUSETTS	12	WASHINGTON	11
MICHIGAN	17	WEST VIRGINIA	5
MINNESOTA	10	WISCONSIN	10
MISSISSIPPI	6	WYOMING	3
MISSOURI	11		

If no presidential candidate wins a majority of electoral votes, the 12th Amendment to the Constitution provides for the presidential election to be decided by the House of Representatives. The House would select the president by majority vote, choosing from the three candidates who received the greatest number of electoral votes. The vote would be taken by state, with each state delegation having one vote. If no vice presidential candidate wins a majority of electoral votes, the Senate would select the vice president by majority vote, with each senator choosing from the two candidates who received the greatest number of electoral votes.

The current workings of the Electoral College are the result of both design and experience. As it now operates:

Each state is allocated a number of electors equal to the number of its U.S. senators (always two) plus the number of its U.S. representatives (which may change each decade according to the size of each state's population as determined in the Census).

- The political parties (or independent candidates) in each state submit to the state's chief election official a list of individuals pledged to their candidate for president and equal in number to the state's electoral vote. Usually, the major political parties select these individuals either in their state party conventions or through appointment by their state party leaders while third parties and independent candidates merely designate theirs.

- Members of Congress and employees of the federal government are prohibited from serving as an elector in order to maintain the balance between the legislative and executive branches of the federal government.
- After their caucuses and primaries, the major parties nominate their candidates for president and vice president in their national conventions, traditionally held in the summer preceding the election. (Third parties and independent candidates follow different procedures according to the individual state laws.) The names of the duly nominated candidates are then officially submitted to each state's chief election official so that they might appear on the general election ballot.
- On the Tuesday following the first Monday of November in years divisible by four, the people in each state cast their ballots for the party slate of electors representing their choice for president and vice president (although as a matter of practice, general election ballots normally say "Electors for" each set of candidates rather than list the individual electors on each slate).
- Whichever party slate wins the most popular votes in the state becomes that state's electors, so that, in effect, whichever presidential ticket gets the most popular votes in a state wins all the electors of that state. The two exceptions to this are Maine and Nebraska where two electors are chosen by statewide popular vote and the remainder by the popular vote within each Congressional district.

- On the Monday following the second Wednesday of December (as established in federal law) each state's electors meet in their respective state capitals and cast their electoral votes — one for president and one for vice president.
- In order to prevent electors from voting only for "favorite sons" of their home state, at least one of their votes must be for a person from outside their state (though this is seldom a problem since the parties have consistently nominated presidential and vice presidential candidates from different states).
- The electoral votes are then sealed and transmitted from each state to the president of the Senate who, on the following January 6, opens and reads them before both houses of Congress.
- The candidate for president with the most electoral votes, provided that it is an absolute majority (more than half of the total), is declared president. Similarly, the vice presidential candidate with the absolute majority of electoral votes is declared vice president.
- In the event no one obtains an absolute majority of electoral votes for president, the U.S. House of Representatives (as the chamber closest to the people) selects the president from among the top three contenders with each state casting only one vote and an absolute majority of the states being required to elect. Similarly, if no one obtains an absolute majority for vice president, then the U.S. Senate makes the selection from among the top two contenders for that office.
- At noon on January 20, the duly elected president and vice president are sworn into office.

Source: Federal Election Commission

2004 Election Timeline

Dates of Presidential Primary Elections, Caucuses, and Nominating Conventions

In the United States, party caucuses and primary elections are essential to choosing presidential candidates. This calendar lists currently scheduled presidential primaries and caucuses leading up to the national 2004 election. (Caucuses are in italics.)

In this context a "caucus" generally refers to a statewide gathering of each party's local political activists during the presidential nomination process. The purpose of the caucus system is to indicate, through delegate choice, which presidential candidate is preferred by each state party's members. Primaries serve a similar function, but they are direct electoral contests held to choose a political party's candidate for a particular public office. Depending on state law, voters cast ballots for the presidential candidate they prefer or for delegates who are "pledged" to support that presidential candidate at the party's convention.

January 19
Iowa

January 27
New Hampshire

February 3
Arizona
Delaware
Missouri
Oklahoma
South Carolina (Democratic)
New Mexico (Democratic)
North Dakota

February 7
Michigan (Democratic)

February 8
Maine (Democratic)

February 10
Tennessee
Virginia
District of Columbia (Republican)

February 14
District of Columbia (Democratic)
Nevada (Democratic)

February 17
Wisconsin

February 24
Utah (Democratic)
Hawaii
Idaho

March 2
California
Connecticut
Georgia
Maryland
Massachusetts
New York
Ohio
Rhode Island
Vermont
Washington
Minnesota

March 9
Florida
Louisiana
Mississippi
Texas

March 13
Kansas (Democratic)

March 16
Illinois

March 20
Alaska (Democratic)

April 13
Colorado (Democratic)

April 27
Pennsylvania

May 4
Indiana
North Carolina

May 6-8
Wyoming (Republican)

May 11
Nebraska
West Virginia

May 15
Wyoming (Democratic)

May 18
Arkansas
Kentucky
Oregon

May 25
Idaho

June 1
Alabama
New Mexico
South Dakota

June 8
Montana
New Jersey

July 26-29
Democratic National
Convention,
Boston

August 30 – September 2
Republican National
Convention,
New York City

November 2, 2004
Election Day

Voter Registration Guide

Before you can vote, you need to register. Registering to vote is a lot like registering for anything else, and it's a simple and easy process. You just give your name, address, and other information to the government office that runs elections where you live – usually a state, county, or city office.

Why do we have to register to vote? Voter registration helps to ensure a fair and orderly democratic system. You register so the government can make sure people vote in the right place and to make sure each person votes just once at each election.

Voting in the right place is important because who you get to vote for depends on where you live. For example, if you live on one street, you may have one set of candidates for the United States Congress; if you live a block over, you may be in a different Congressional District and be voting for a different set of candidates.Usually the people in a precinct go to vote in the same location, usually a public place like a school or a church. Most voting districts are pretty small (the size of a neighborhood) though in rural areas a district can stretch for miles.

Who Can Register?

To register in any state, you need to be a U.S. citizen, 18 or older by the next election, and a resident of the state. You can't be a felon and you can't be mentally incompetent. In a few places, you can vote in local elections even if you are not a U.S. citizen. To check the rules for your state, call your state's elections office.

Some people may not be sure where to register to vote. This is often true of college students, whose families live in one place and who go to school somewhere else. Usually, those students can legally register in either place; it depends on where you feel your residence is.

How to Register

The rules on registering to vote vary between states, counties, and cities. But there are some rules that apply everywhere: for example, under the "Motor Voter" law, motor vehicle offices must offer voter registration.

Generally, there are a few ways to register.

1. **At motor vehicle and other government offices**
   You can usually register in motor vehicle offices, public assistance offices, agencies that help people with disabilities, public libraries, and other public buildings.

2. **Registering by mail**
   You don't have to wait until your next trip to the Department of Motor Vehicles. You can start the process of registering by mail. Although it may not be required, it is a good idea to include a copy of your photo ID with your voter registration application when you mail it in. You can call your local elections office and ask them to send you a voter registration application in the mail. Just fill it out and send it back.

3. **Get started online**
   Although you can now start the registration process online, you cannot actually register online, and a few states won't yet accept the "universal" mail-in form; instead, when they get that form they will send you a state form which you then have to fill out and mail in. You'll get registered anyway — it just means an extra step. There are several sites to help you register to vote including www.justvote.org, www.yourvotematters.org, www.declareyourself.com, and www.lww.org.

4. **At the elections office**
   The traditional way to register is to go to a local board of elections office or county courthouse and fill out a form.

5. **In public places**
   Sometimes, especially when elections are coming up, you may find volunteers at tables in public places offering to register you. These may be at colleges, churches, fairs, or other places where people gather.

The Registration Form

If you get a registration form from your state, county, or city, we can't tell you exactly what it will look like. That's because each place has a slightly different form.

The form will ask for your name, address, date of birth, and proof of U.S. citizenship. You also have to give your driver's license number, if you have a license, or the last four digits of your Social Security number. If you don't have either a driver's license or a Social Security number, the state will assign you a voter identification number. These numbers are to help the state keep track of voters. Check the form carefully, including the back, to see the rules for the place where you live.

If you want to make sure that you get properly registered, do these three things:

- Fill out the form accurately and completely, and try to make sure people can read it.
- Register early if you can – say, right after you move to a new place. Avoid the pre-election rush.
- If you don't hear from the elections office within three weeks, call to find out what's happening with your registration.

Within a few weeks after you send in or hand in your registration application, you should get a notice in the mail telling you that you are now officially a registered voter. Hold on to that notice. Often those notices tell you where to go to vote, and that's something you'll want to know later on.

Source: Some of this information was obtained from the Federal Election Commission.

State Voter Registration Deadlines

STATE	REGISTRATION DEADLINES FOR ALL ELECTIONS
Alabama	10 days before an election.
Alaska	30 days before an election.
Arizona	29 days before an election.
Arkansas	30 days before an election.
California	29 days before an election.
Colorado	29 days before an election. If the application is received in the mail without a postmark, it must be received within five days of the close of registration.
Connecticut	14 days before an election.
Delaware	20 days prior to the general election and 21 days prior to any primary election.
D.C.	30 days before an election.
Florida	29 days before an election.
Georgia	The fifth Monday before a general primary, general election, or presidential preference primary. The fifth day after the date of the call for all other special primaries and special elections.
Hawaii	30 days before an election.
Idaho	25 days before an election — mail; 24 days for in person; or Election Day at the polls.
Illinois	29 days before primary; 28 days before a general election.
Indiana	29 days before an election.

Iowa	Delivered by 5 p.m. 10 days before a state primary or general election; 11 days before all others. A postmark 15 or more days before an election is considered on time.
Kansas	Delivered 15 days before an election.
Kentucky	28 days before an election.
Louisiana	24 days before an election.
Maine	10 business days before an election or delivered in person up to and including Election Day.
Maryland	9 p.m. on the fifth Monday before an election.
Massachusetts	20 days before an election.
Michigan	30 days before an election.
Minnesota	Delivered by 5 p.m. 21 days before an election; also Election Day registration at polling places.
Mississippi	30 days before an election.
Missouri	28 days before an election.
Montana	30 days before an election.
Nebraska	The fourth Tuesday before an election or delivered by 6 p.m. on the second Friday before an election.
Nevada	9 p.m. on the fifth Saturday before any primary or general election; 9 p.m. on the third Saturday before any recall or special election unless held on the same day as a primary or general election. Then it remains the fifth Saturday.
New Hampshire	Must be received by city or town clerk 10 days before an election; or register

	at the polls on Election Day.
New Jersey	29 days before an election.
New Mexico	28 days before an election.
New York	25 days before an election.
North Carolina	Postmarked 25 days before an election or received in the elections office or designated voter registration agency by 5 p.m.
North Dakota	North Dakota does not have voter registration.
Ohio	30 days before an election.
Oklahoma	25 days before an election.
Oregon	21 days before an election. (There is no deadline for applications for change of name, change of address, or to register with a party.)
Pennsylvania	30 days before an election.
Rhode Island	30 days before an election. *Check Saturday hours.
South Carolina	30 days before an election.
South Dakota	Delivered 15 days before an election.
Tennessee	30 days before an election.
Texas	30 days before an election.
Utah	20 days before an election.
Vermont	Delivered to the town clerk before noon, postmarked or submitted to DMV on the second Saturday before an election.
Virginia	Delivered 29 days before an election.
Washington	30 days before an election; or delivered in-person up to 15 days before an

	election at a location designated by the county elections officer (usually the county courthouse).
West Virginia	30 days before an election.
Wisconsin	13 days before an election; or completed in the local voter registration office one day before an election; or completed at the polling place on Election Day.
Wyoming	30 days before an election, or register at the polling place on Election Day.

Glossary of Terms for the 2004 Elections

Ballot - The official list of all candidates and issues upon which a voter is entitled to vote at an election. You receive the ballot at your polling place or when you vote by absentee ballot.

Campaign - An activity undertaken to persuade voters to vote for a candidate or for or against a ballot issue.

Candidate - An individual who seeks election to an office.

Canvassing - Canvassing is the process of examining ballots or groups of ballots, subtotals, and cumulative totals in order to determine the official returns of, and prepare the certification for, a primary or general election.

Canvassing Board - A board used to certify all election returns. It consists of the county auditor, county prosecuting attorney, and the chairman of the county legislative authority.

Caucus - Literally, it means "a meeting," and it is one of the main mechanisms used by modern American political parties to nominate their candidate for president. In the presidential nomination process, it now denotes a meeting of local party activists at the precinct level who select, in an open forum, delegates to county meetings. These delegates in turn select delegates to state meetings, and these state-level conventions select delegates to the party's national convention.

Chad - A term made famous by the November 2000 presidential election. A chad is the tiny piece of ballot material that should be detached from a punch card ballot when a person votes.

Congress - The national legislative assembly of the United States, consisting of the House of Representatives and the Senate.

Constituency - A body of voters in a jurisdiction having the right to take part in the election of a candidate.

Constitution - The document that lays out the basic framework for organizing and granting powers to a government. We have a State Constitution for each state and a U.S. Constitution.

Democracy - Government or rule by the people.

District - A subdivision of a state county, city, or other unit of local government.

Elected Official - An individual serving in a public capacity who obtained the position through an election.

Election - The right or ability to choose a government official or policy.

Election Board - A group of election officers working at a precinct or groups of precincts in a polling place on Election Day.

Election Officer - Any officer who has a duty to perform relating to elections under the provisions of any statute, charter, or ordinance.

Electoral College - The body of state-selected delegates that officially elects the president of the United States.

Electorate - A body of registered voters eligible to vote in an election.

Exit Poll - A poll or survey conducted on individuals after they have finished voting and are leaving their polling location. Exit polls are often used to predict who is going to win an election.

Federal Election Commission (FEC) - A 1974 amendment to the Federal Election Campaign Act established the FEC to enforce federal campaign finance laws during an election campaign. A small section of the FEC, the Office of Election Administration, works with state and local election officials on election administration issues.

Federal Post Card Application (FPCA) - A form provided pursuant to federal law to members of the U.S. armed forces and merchant marines, their dependents, and other U.S. citizens abroad to allow them to request an absentee ballot and, if necessary, to register to vote temporarily.

Federal Write-In Absentee Ballot (FWAB) - A special form that may be used by members of the military and the merchant marines, their family members, and certain other Americans living abroad. This form facilitates the voter registration and absentee voting process.

Filing Fee - A fee paid at the time a candidate files a declaration of candidacy to be placed on a ballot.

Filing Officer - The county or state elections officer with whom declarations of candidacy for an office are filed.

Filing Period - A time period used to file declarations of candidacy.

General Election - The election held the first Tuesday after the first Monday in November of each year.

Gerrymander - Setting the boundary for a political district so that it advantages one particular political party.

Inactive Voter - A person who is registered to vote but has not voted in a number of elections and has had an official election mailing returned undeliverable to the local election official is placed in an inactive status.

Inauguration - The event that marks the transfer of power to a newly elected official.

Incumbent - The person who holds an office, either by election or appointment.

Independent - A person not affiliated with a political party.

Legislature - The branch of government that makes laws.

Levy Election - A tax to be voted on at an election.

Lobby - To attempt to influence politics in favor of a special interest.

Majority - To obtain a majority of votes is to receive at least 50 percent plus one.

Measure - A question or proposal submitted in an election to obtain the voters' will on the matter.

Midterm elections - This term refers to elections held in-between presidential elections – that is, two years after the previous, and two years before the next presidential elections. Each midterm election selects one-third of the 100 members of the U.S. Senate and all 435 members of the House of Representatives, as well as many state and local officials.

Motor Voter - The nickname for the part of the National Voter Registration Act of 1993 that required states to offer voter registration at driver's licensing and other government offices.

National Voter Registration Act (NVRA) - Frequently referred to as the "motor voter law," this 1993 federal law requires that states allow residents to obtain voter registration materials as they apply for a driver's license as well as utilize given public services.

Non-partisan Offices - Certain elective public offices are filled on a non-partisan basis, which means that the candidates vie for the position without any indication of a political party affiliation.

Office - A specific position to which people seek election. Each office has specific duties and powers.

Official - An individual serving in a public capacity.

Optical Scan Ballot - A paper ballot that requires voters to use a special marking device to either fill in a bubble or connect two arrows in order to cast a vote. Once the ballots are marked, they are inserted into a special counting machine that reads the markings and tabulates the votes.

Over Vote - An over vote occurs in an instance where the number of votes cast by a voter for an office on the ballot exceeds the number of candidates to be advanced or elected to the office. In such instances, no votes cast for the office are counted.

Paper Ballot - A paper ballot system employs uniform official ballots of various stock weight on which the names of all candidates and issues are printed. Voters record their choices, in private, by marking the boxes next to the candidate or issue choice they select and drop the voted ballot in a sealed ballot box.

Partisan Office - Certain elective public offices are filled on a partisan basis, which means that the candidates vie for the position on the basis of political party affiliation.

Petition - The form used for collecting signatures of registered voters for certifying an initiative or referendum.

Platform - A formal statement of position on major political issues drafted by a candidate or a political party. In other countries, the "platform" may be called the party "manifesto." The major parties ratify their platforms at their national conventions.

Plurality - To receive one more vote than the next highest vote-getter.

Political Action Committee (PAC) - A business, union, or organization that forms a committee and contributes funds to a candidate.

Political Party - A group that shares the same views about government and works together to win elections.

Politics - The art or science of government.

Polling Place - The place where you vote on Election Day (polling means voting).

Precinct - A geographical subdivision for voting purposes.

Presidential Elector - An individual selected as a member of a political party and pledged to cast a vote for a certain presidential candidate.

Primary – An electoral contest held to determine each political party's candidate for a particular public office. Primaries may be held at all levels of government, including local contests for mayor, district races for the U.S. House of Representatives, statewide elections for governor or U.S. senator, and president of the United States. Primaries for presidential candidates are held at the state level to indicate who the people of that state prefer to be the parties' candidates. Depending on state law, voters cast ballots directly for the presidential candidate they prefer or for delegates who are "pledged" to support that presidential candidate at convention time.

Proposition - A measure that is presented to the public to vote on.

Punchcard Voting System - Punchcard systems employ a card (or cards) and a small clipboard-sized device for recording votes. Voters punch holes in the cards (with a supplied punch device) opposite their candidate or ballot issue choice. After voting, the voter may place the ballot in a ballot box, or the ballot may be fed into a computer vote-tabulating device at the precinct.

Redistricting - The process that occurs every ten years after the Census for adjusting political boundaries to ensure equal representation for various districts and political subdivisions.

Referendum Bills - Referendum bills are proposed laws referred to the electorate by the legislature

Referendum Measures - Referendum measures are laws recently passed by the legislature that are placed on the ballot because of petitions signed by voters.

Registered Voter - A registered voter is an individual who is a citizen of the United States, 18 years of age, and a legal resident of the United States who has properly filled out a registration form and been placed on the list of voters by an elections official.

Sample Ballot - A printed facsimile of all the issues and offices on the ballot.

Sound Bite - A brief, very quotable remark by a candidate for office that is repeated on radio and television news programs.

Straw Poll - In modern presidential politics, a *non-binding* vote, often taken among party activists and usually at a very early stage in a candidate-selection process, to indicate which candidate or candidates are preferred by a local group.

Swing Voters - Voters not loyal to a particular political party, usually independents, who can determine the outcome of an election by "swinging" one way or the other on an issue or candidate, often reversing their choices the next time around.

Ticket Splitting - Voting for candidates of different political parties in the same election — say, voting for a Democrat for president and a Republican for senator. Because ticket splitters do not vote for all of one party's candidates, they are said to "split" their votes.

Veto - The power of the governor to prevent a bill that has been passed by the legislature from becoming a law. With a supermajority the legislature can override a governor's veto.

Voter Registration - Having your name on the official list of voters. You must be registered using your legal residence as your address.

Voter Turnout - The number of people who voted in an election. Often expressed as a percentage of registered voters who cast ballots.

Voters Pamphlet - A pamphlet produced by an elections official that provides information about ballot measures, candidates, and other elections information.

Voting - Making your choices of candidates, and yes or no for any questions, on the official ballot.

How To Contact Your State Election Officials

If you have questions about how to register to vote, how to register other people to vote, where to vote, or any other question about the election, contact your state election office:

Alabama
Elections Division
(334) 242-7210
www.sos.state.al.us

Alaska
Election Services
(907) 465-4611
www.gov.state.ak.us/ltgov/elections/homepage.html

Arizona
Election Services
(602) 542-8683
www.sosaz.com

Arkansas
Elections Department
(501) 682-3419
www.sosweb.state.ar.us

California
Election Division
(916) 657-2166
www.ss.ca.gov

Colorado
Elections Center
(303) 894-2200
www.sos.state.co.us

Connecticut
Elections Office
(860) 509-6100
www.sots.state.ct.us

Delaware
Election Commissioner
(800) 273-9500
www.state.de.us/election/

District of Columbia
Board of Elections
(202) 727-2525
www.dcboee.org/

Florida
Division of Elections
(850) 245-6200
www.dos.state.fl.us/

Georgia
Elections Division
(404) 656-2871
www.sos.state.ga.us

Hawaii
Office of Elections
(808) 453-8683
http://www.hawaii.gov/elections/

Idaho
Secretary of State
(208) 334-2300
www.idsos.state.id.us

Illinois
Board of Elections
(217) 782-4141,
(312) 814-6440
http://www.elections.state.il.us/

Indiana
Elections Division
(317) 232-3939
www.in.gov/sos

Iowa
Secretary of State,
Voter/Elections Center
(515) 281-5865
www.sos.state.ia.us

Kansas
Elections and Legislative Matters Division
(785) 296-4561
www.kssos.org

Kentucky
State Board of Elections
(502) 573-7100
www.sos.state.ky.us

Louisiana
Elections Division
(225) 342-4970
www.sec.state.la.us

Maine
Division of Elections
(207) 624-7650
www.state.me.us/sos

Maryland
State Board of Elections
(410) 269-2840
www.elections.state.md.us

Massachusetts
Elections Division
(617) 727-2828
www.state.ma.us/sec

Michigan
Bureau of Elections
(517) 373-2540
www.michigan.gov/sos

Minnesota
Secretary of State
(651) 251-1440 (metro area)
1-877-600-8683 (outside metro area)
www.state.mn.us/ebranch/sos

Mississippi
Elections Division
(601) 359-6359
www.sos.state.ms.us

Missouri
Secretary of State
(573) 751-2301 or
(800) 669-8683
www.sos.mo.gov

Montana
Elections and Legislative Bureau
(406) 444-4732
1-888-884-8683
http://sos.state.mt.us

Nebraska
Secretary of State
(402) 471-3229
www.nol.org/home/SOS

Nevada
Elections Division
(775) 684-5705
http://sos.state.nv.us

New Hampshire
Election Division
(603) 271-3242
http://webster.state.nh.us/sos

New Jersey
Division of Elections
(609) 292-3760
www.state.nj.us/lps/elections/electionshome.html

New Mexico
Bureau of Elections
(505) 827-3600
www.sos.state.nm.us

New York
Board of Elections
(518) 474-6220
www.elections.state.ny.us/

North Carolina
Board of Elections
(919) 733-7173
www.sboe.state.nc.us

North Dakota
Elections Office
(701) 328-4146
www.state.nd.us/sec

Ohio
Secretary of State
(614) 466-2585
www.state.oh.us/sos

Oklahoma
State Elections Board
(405) 521-2391
www.state.ok.us/~elections/index.html

Oregon
Elections Division
(503) 986-1518
www.sos.state.or.us

Pennsylvania
Commissioner of Elections
(717) 787-5280
www.dos.state.pa.us

Rhode Island
Elections Division
(401) 222-2340
www.state.ri.us/

South Carolina
Election Commission
(803) 734-9060
www.state.sc.us/scsec/

South Dakota
Elections
(605) 773-3537
www.sdsos.gov

Tennessee
Division of Elections
(615) 741-7956
www.state.tn.us/sos/

Texas
Elections Division
(512) 463-5650 or
(800) 252-8683
www.sos.state.tx.us/

Utah
Elections Office
(801) 538-1041 or
1-800-995-8683
http://elections.utah.gov/

Vermont
Elections Division
(802) 828-2363
www.sec.state.vt.us/

Virginia
State Board of Elections
(804) 786-6551
www.sbe.state.va.us

Washington
Secretary of State
(360) 902-4180
www.secstate.wa.gov

West Virginia
Secretary of State
(304) 558-6000
www.wvsos.com

Wisconsin
State Elections Board
(608) 266-8005
http://elections.state.wi.us

Wyoming
Election Administration
(307) 777-7640
http://soswy.state.wy.us